Dressing *the* *petite* woman

by Ellen York

petite

when *great* things come in small packages

Dressing the Petite Woman
Copyright 2006

Produced by: Fitting Images, Everett, WA
Graphic Design: Kathleen Stimmel; Amie Ross
Photography: Wendy Grace; Joshua Kramer
Editing: Carolyn Acheson

ELLEN YORK IMAGE INSTITUTE

Ellen York Image Institute
P.O. Box 27439
Seattle, WA 98165-2439
www.ellenyork.com

ISBN: 0-9772764-0-6
Printed in the United States of America
First Printing: 2006
Sunset Press, Kent, WA

Foreword

The essence of Ellen York resonates in this book, radiating her effervescent spirit, gusto, and guts. A bright, multitalented women, when Ellen takes on a commitment, she does it right. Whether she's trying to find just the right wardrobe for that hard-to-please, everyday client, or to convince a 6'5" athletic-hunk celebrity to adopt some social graces, or to reach out to readers everywhere through a book like this one, she gets the job done.

I've known Ellen going on twenty years, and it's an honor to introduce her here. As a volunteer on our Career and Technical Education Advisory Committee, she is a tireless and respected leader in business and her community. I applaud her approach—clear, plain-spoken, wise. She looks inward to look outward toward others.

Ellen does it all with common sense and humor. Oh, yes—and decades of education, knowledge, and hands-on experience. She's a good listener, too, and truly interested in you. She cuts to the chase: "What do you need?" and "What can I do for you?" She's down to earth, and her wit makes her suggestions welcome. She's a fixer, a problem-solver. Her advice and expertise will improve your self-image—again and again.

"What will *Dressing the Petite Woman* do for me?" I thought, before I delved into this book. How can I look taller, slimmer, more stylish? With my 5'2" frame, I was in familiar territory. Ellen's words offered awareness, insight, and, best of all, advice that I could apply myself. I felt her mentoring every step of the way, and recalled a quote:

What we nurture in ourselves will grow; that is nature's eternal law.
—*Anonymous*

Don't let Ellen's spunky spontaneity fool you. She knows of what she speaks! Her vitality spills over into everything she does, and she makes it fun. Her simple, effective techniques will enable you to radiate your best self. Ellen encourages you to project your best you. I can hear her saying, "Knock 'em dead, kid!"

After reading this book, you will feel refreshed and look great. She has cleared the way. Read between the lines and catch her spirit!

I celebrate myself, and sing myself.
—*From Song of Myself, by Walt Whitman*

Sandra J. Fredric, MA Ed.
Secondary Educator
Work-based Learning Coordinator

Contents

ELLEN YORK IMAGE INSTITUTE

ELLEN YORK IMAGE INSTITUTE

To the loves of my life, my grandchildren
Hayley and Parker

Introduction

Introduction

The thought of shopping and pulling a new look together is a real challenge to many women. You probably have put it off because you can't stand shopping. Or maybe your life is so busy that you can't justify the time. Perhaps you don't like how you look and find trying on clothes frustrating and depressing.

Good news! Reading this book will start you on a pleasant journey toward the NEW YOU. Your self-esteem will start to rise, and you'll begin to take pleasure in looking at yourself in the mirror.

First, repeat my motto:
There is no such thing as a perfect body.
Then start reading....

You will learn to select blouses, tops, jackets, dresses, pants, skirts, and evening wear that will flatter your shape. You will find out which colors accentuate your eyes, hair color, and skin tone and present you at your best. You will get out of the trap of black, black, black and dazzle your friends and family with colors that look beautiful on you. You will have fun accessorizing with the shoes, jewelry, belts, handbags, scarves, ponchos, and hats that reveal your personality.

ELLEN YORK IMAGE INSTITUTE

Highlight, underline, make notes, and circle information and photos that pertain to you and your wonderful body. Then take the plunge. You'll make some mistakes along the way, but that's all part of learning how to present your best self. Enjoy the *NEW YOU* that's ready to come out and show itself to the world!

—Ellen York

The suggestions in this book will help you better dress the body you have. With photographs of different-shaped models showing "before and after" looks, and a myriad of clothing styles, you'll begin to see how you, too, can dress with style and look fantastic!

Are you
5'4"
and under?

If so, your aim is to look . . .

taller.

And if you are at your ideal weight
or heavier, you will want to . . .

minimize your weight.

You can achieve these goals through
better clothing styles and color choices.
At the same time, through wise clothing
selection, you can camouflage the areas
of your body you'd rather not showcase.

When you look at yourself sideways, you'll immediately see
the areas you want to camouflage. The model here will want to
minimize her bust, upper arms, and hips. Pants or skirts that glide
over the hip and thigh will make the short body appear taller, too.

Now the eye captures the look of a woman proportioned much differently than the same model to the left. The looser-fitting T-shirt de-emphasizes her bustline; the sporty jacket has enough room in the sleeves to hide her upper arms; and the pants drop over the thighs with ease. Voila! What a fit!

In all my years as a dress designer and image consultant, I have never seen a perfect body. As you will find out, the secrets in this book will help you. . .

accentuate
the positive

and de-emphasize the negative.

When I select clothing for a client, a common response is, "I would never have picked this for myself!" And that's why this book was conceived.

"I have never seen a perfect body!"

Knowing your
best colors

Knowing your best colors

The first thing I do with clients is to color-drape them to see what colors look best next to their face. Your best colors will enhance your hair, eye color, and skin tone. You'll wear either warm colors or cool colors. Read on and look at some of the colors best worn by each "season."

You most likely won't have color drapes for each season, so you may use pieces of fabric, pillowcases, placemats, or pillows. While in a store, hold different colored T-shirts up to your face. Look for colors that don't drain all the color from your face, and colors that don't contrast sharply, such as too bright. Colors should add richness to your cheeks and show off your eyes.

When you wear your best colors, people will notice you, not your bright red dress. When you wear colors next to your face, they should flatter your skin and eyes. Perhaps you need a few highlights in your hair to give it some life. Talk to your hair dresser about this.

You might really like a dress or jacket you see in a store, but the color may look awful on you. Wearing your best colors can be an asset in any setting and will have a lot to do with your appeal and success. You will be advertising your good taste.

Color palettes

Some time ago, a concept of color was developed relating to the seasons of the year. This has proved to be a popular way of classifying people according to their best colors. Some clients can back up a season or move forward to the next one and find a few colors that look good. In the following pages you will learn how to discover your season and get out of your "color ruts." It will lessen your frustration in clothes shopping because you will pass up colors that aren't part of your color palette.

TIP:

If you have an image consultant in your area, you might want to invest in a color consultation. You will get swatches of your color palette and have a whole lot of fun finding out what colors look best on you. By the way, these colors apply to make-up, too.

Knowing your best colors will open a whole new world and shorten your shopping time, too.

The Winter person gets to wear black, white, magenta, fuchsia, sapphire blue, emerald green, and purple—all the jewel tones.

winter

If you are a Winter of the Caucasian race, your eyes may be blue, steely blue, green, or brown. Your hair is black or dark brown, rarely blond, and never red or auburn. Your complexion is porcelain, almost white. Men who are Winters can have an almost blue beard. Alas, Winters have a blue undertone to their skin. If your skin has an olive tone, you'll soon realize you can pull off a few autumn colors, too.

If you are African-American, Asian-American, Native-American Indian, Hispanic, or simply dark-skinned, you, too, are most likely to be a Winter. There are more Winters in the world than any other season. On occasion, I've determined that a dark-skinned person is an Autumn—rare but possible. In these instances, the skin is more brown than black, the eyes are hazel, and the hair is very dark brown, not black.

A Winter looks stunning in cherry red—a red with a definite blue undertone. (Hold cherry red next to an orange-red or tomato red, and you'll see the difference.) You're able to wear turquoise blue, as well as navy and midnight blue.

A note of caution to Winters: Just because you are able to wear black, don't get hung up on black, black, black when you have so many terrific colors to choose from. You will want to own a black dress and a black suit (pants and/or skirt), but open your mind to the vivid colors that you can wear next to your face. Black and white are easy, but you have many other color options. Try fuchsia, turquoise blue, purple, a deep dark green, and navy blue.

When a beautiful dress comes along in magenta, buy it! When you see a royal blue silk blouse or knit top, purchase it to wear under a jacket. The jewel-tone colors are beautiful next to your skin. They give life to your face and sparkle to your eyes. If you try to wear Summer, Autumn or Spring colors, you'll look washed out or the colors will clash with your skin tone.

A Winter is the only season that can "legally" wear black and white. The rest of us wear varying shades of navy and off-white.

The best jewelry tone for a Winter is silver. Pewtered and hammered pieces are good, and pearls with gold soften the gold.

Famous Winters: *Courteney Cox Arquette, Star Jones*

A Winter looks stunning in cherry red, and when a beautiful dress comes along in magenta, buy it!

summer

The best colors for a Summer are the muted tones of a Winter. Pinks and mauves, taupe and eggplant, light blue, navy blue, seafoam green—colors like these show off the skin, eyes, and hair to their best advantage.

Summers have a pink undertone to their skin. Eyes may be blue, gray-blue, green, gray, or gray-green. Hair is light brown, medium brown, blond, or dishwater blond.

Navy and brown are "blacks" for Summers. Off-white substitutes for white. Hold a stark white shirt next to your face and look in the mirror. Now hold up a piece of fabric in off-white. Notice the difference. Do the same with black, then navy blue. Now you're starting to get it. The off-white and navy are much better next to your face, creating less of a contrast and bringing out your skin color.

Please forgive Summers for owning some white T-shirts and a couple of white blouses. At times a pretty scarf can provide the needed color next to your face. To enhance your wardrobe, purchase some off-white, ivory, or cream-colored blouses and knit tops.

Sweaters, blouses, knit tops—even suits and dresses—can be found in lovely shades of taupe and eggplant. Light blue shows off blue eyes and doesn't overpower the pink undertone of the skin. Seafoam green may turn your eyes from gray to green. Gray with a hint of blue is fine, too.

TIP: *If your hair is mousy brown, have your hair dresser foil different shades of blond to highlight your face.*

The best jewelry tone for a Summer is silver. Pewtered and hammered choices are nice, and pearls with gold soften the gold.

Famous Summers: *Renee Zelwegger, Calista Flockhart*

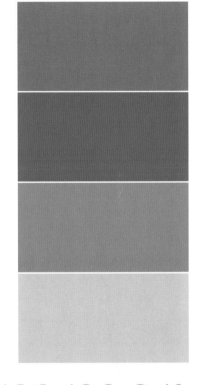

summer

The best colors for a Summer are the muted tones of a Winter.

An Autumn relates to my favorite season of the year, with the beautiful colors of the earth and the changing colors of leaves on the trees.

autumn

The undertone of your skin is golden, and you are likely to have freckles, perhaps a ruddy complexion, and coarse hair. Your eyes might be hazel, brown with gold flecks, golden brown, chestnut, green, or gray-blue, often with a dark circle around the pupil. Your hair will undoubtedly have red highlights and could be auburn, red, rich dark brown, or golden brown.

As with any season, you'll find that you wear some of the autumn colors better than others. As you put autumn colors next to your face, you'll see the color of your eyes standing out, or the color will enhance your skin tone. A color should complement your hair color as well. A trip to the hair dresser might do the trick with foil streaks of auburn or gold.

Colors you'll be putting next to your face are tomato red, olive, rust, different shades of brown, a rich, deep gold, emerald green, deep green, camel, purple, turquoise with a

yellow or gold cast, navy, shell (with a gold cast), salmon, and burgundy. Autumns can get hung up on black just like the other seasons do. Instead, think about your "new black" as navy, a textured olive, or a rich dark brown. Look for animal prints in a scarf or blouse—even a two-piece dress. If your choice for a suit is black, look at Autumns' enticing color options for blouses and knit tops that will go underneath the jacket.

Your jewelry will be gold, and accessorizing can be fun. Choose beaded jewelry with bead colors that pick up your eye and hair color. You'll soon begin to see everything that autumn has to offer in color.

The texture of Autumn can be the tweed of a jacket and skirt, or it might be ribbing in a knit top and herringbone in the pant fabric. When dressing for the holidays, Autumns should be on the lookout for a stretchy velvet in dark brown or olive.

Make your shopping easier by purchasing pants in colors that will be easy to find tops for—for instance, pants in different shades of brown, camel, or dark olive. Black pants can work because you'll be able to find colorful Autumn tops in solid colors as well as patterns.

Famous Autumns: *Susan Sarandon, Debra Messing*

You'll start seeing yourself come alive in autumn colors!

If you have skin like peaches and cream (the most beautiful complexion), you are likely a Spring. These lucky ladies get to wear clear, bright colors with a yellow undertone.

When I close my eyes, I see a Spring and all the colors she can wear! Some Springs look better in the pastel shades, and others excel in the darker shades.

Unlike Autumns, who look good in the more muted shades, Springs can wear cadet blue, fire-engine red, light and brighter yellows, light blue, and yellow-turquoise (not blue-turquoise), light and brighter pinks, purple and lavender, mint green, and dark green. Coral and salmon will likely be gorgeous on you.

Depending on what you wear, your eyes may be bright blue, gray, light green, or green that turns blue. You may have brown or hazel eyes with yellow specks. Like Autumns, the eyes of Springs often have a dark circle around the pupil.

Your hair may be strawberry blond or red, or sometimes almost orange. Or you may be blond or have blond hair with red highlights. You probably were a towhead (white-haired) as a child.

A Spring gets to wear clear, bright colors with a yellow undertone.

ELLEN YORK IMAGE INSTITUTE

TIP: *The best jewelry tone for Spring and Autumn is gold, not shiny, but hammered or pewtered. It looks more expensive, never inexpensive.*

Famous Springs: *Nicole Kidman, Barbara Walters*

spring

TIP:

If you are African-American, Asian-American, Native-American Indian, Hispanic, or simply dark-skinned, you are most likely to be a Winter.

As a Winter, don't forget the jewel tones that look so beautiful on you. They're a nice change from black and white.

winter

Hair:
Black or dark brown, rarely blond, and never red or auburn.

Eyes:
Blue, steely blue, green, or brown.

Complexion:
Asian or African American skin is dark. Caucasian skin may be porcelain or appear rosy-cheeked. You may have olive skin, which means you'll be able to wear a few Autumn colors, but not all.

summer

Hair:
Light brown, dishwater blond, or medium brown. Sometimes dark brown.

Eyes:
Blue, gray-blue, green, gray, or gray-green.

Complexion:
Pink undertone to skin. Tans easily in the summer.

autumn

Hair:
Auburn, red, rich dark brown, or golden brown, red highlights.

Eyes:
Hazel, brown with gold flecks, golden brown, chestnut, green, or gray-blue. Look for a dark circle around the pupil.

Complexion:
Undertone is golden. Skin may appear ruddy. You're likely to have freckles, and you blush easily.

spring

Hair:
Strawberry blond, red, almost orange, blond, or blond with red highlights.

Eyes:
Bright blue, gray, light green, or green that turns blue. Yellow specks in brown and hazel eyes. Look for a dark circle around the pupil.

Complexion:
Peaches and cream. Look for freckles. You blush easily.

A closet inventory

A closet inventory

As soon as you know what colors are right for you, it's time to do a closet inventory. You won't want to come home from shopping for the *new you* and have no space for your new duds!

I'll bet a lot of you have one or more closets crammed and jammed with old, outdated, wrong-colored, ill-fitting clothes, and sale items with the price tags still attached.

A closet inventory means weeding out clothes you no longer wear:

- clothes that no longer fit
- clothes that look worn out
- clothes you thought were a great idea at the time but you never wear
- clothes in a color that looks awful on you
- clothes in a style that would look good on someone else—but not you
- clothes that are clearly out of date. By the time they come back in style, the fabrics will be better, and they won't be in exactly the same style.

Make them gone—get them out of your closet!

Now you have room in your closet.
Read on, ladies, and let's have some fun!

A Closet Inventory

Now, make three piles:

- Clothes to give away.

- Clothes still in good shape that can go to consignment or charity.

- Clothes that can be tossed out or cut up for rags (yes, some are that bad!).

TIP: *Large garbage bags with handles are ideal for this job. They hold a lot and are easy to carry. Be brave— buy several boxes of them.*

You're going to create a wardrobe that requires planning and some serious work. Be as objective as you can about your body shape, personality, lifestyle, and career. All of these will factor into the clothes you buy. This is the time to start opening your mind to new styles and clothes that will enhance your attributes and camouflage the parts of your body you don't want people to notice. This long overdue makeover will get you out of a rut you've probably been in for quite some time.

- As an Image Consultant and former dress designer—*I've never seen a perfect body—NEVER.* So give yourself five minutes to beat up on yourself for not having the perfect body, then go forward. You will be looking for tops, jackets, pants, and skirts with cuts and necklines that enhance your look.

- I'm built straight up and down. I don't have a small waist, so it's always a challenge for me to find skirts and pants that are big enough in the waist. Pants and skirts cut slightly below the waist fit me better.

- You want styles that complement your body type, not draw attention to a pooched tummy, a large waist, either tiny or large breasts, and hips you'd rather not display. Flattering clothes await you.

- Take notes, and make a budget for now, plus one for each upcoming month for the next 6 months.

That way, you won't put yourself in debt to the credit card company. Over-spending can defeat your plan. Try not to sink back into impulse buying or buying something just because it's on sale. Take it a step at a time, and get used to the *new you*.

- You're not building a wardrobe totally from scratch. You've got some clothes left after your closet inventory that will work and blend in with your new purchases. Six months from now you can start letting some older pieces go as you replace them with new clothing.

- A thorough closet inventory can take a weekend, or even longer. Get your discards out of the house and immediately into your car. Otherwise they have a tendency to crawl right back into your closet!

- A closet cleansing is good for your health. You'll feel like a load has been lifted from your shoulders. And it has!

Get your discards out of the house and into your car. Otherwise they have a tendency to crawl right back into your closet!

Have someone take your measurements as follows:

1. **Bust size:** Measure around your back and over the fullest part of your breasts.

2. **Shoulder width:** Measure 4" down from the back of the neck. Stretch the tape measure from shoulder to shoulder where a set-in sleeveline would be.

3. **Hip:** Measure down from the waistline to the fullest part of the hip, and then measure all the way around. You'll be looking for pants that are cut with a longer crotch to compensate for the low-slung fuller hip. No hip? A pant cut with a shorter crotch should work well.

4. *Tummy:* Measure 4" down from waist, side to side. This will tell you how much or how little you'll need in the front of the pants. Giving this information to the salesperson will aid her in showing you the brands that are cut with room in the front. Age has a lot to do with tummy problems, and the signs of childbearing become obvious at menopause.

5. *Thighs:* Measure around the leg at the top. Do you have bird legs or fuller legs? This is information for the salesperson to have so she can direct you to pants that have a fuller upper-leg cut. Those with bird legs can try on pants with a slimmer leg cut.

6. *Length of leg:* Measure down from the waist on the outside of the leg to the floor, without shoes. For the inside seam, measure from the very top inside leg down to the floor.

7. *Crotch measurement:* Measure from the waist in front, under the crotch and up to the waistline in back.

Petite departments

Petite departments

For your height and weight, shopping in the Petite section of department stores is advisable. If you've tried to buy Misses sizes and have been unhappy with the fit—for instance, the crotch hangs too low and the knit tops and blouses are too long—it's time to try out the Petite department. Petite clothes are cut differently than Misses clothes, in keeping with the height and proportions of the shorter woman. Most women of Petite height and weight will split their time between Petite and Misses departments—unless you're 5'2" and shorter. Then your buying will be mostly in Petites.

- The jacket in Petite sizes is shorter, with your height in mind. Petite pants are cut shorter in the leg and shorter in the crotch. The waist, tummy, and hips are cut according to the petite women's average measurements. Blouses and tops are shorter, as are sleeves. In larger Petite sizes, blouses and tops have more room in the front to allow for a larger bust, and are larger in the arms. The back typically has more room, too.

- You may have to try on several brands before you find a winning fit. Not all styles will fit you well or offer the look you want, but at least you're in the right department. Keep in mind that you can have sleeves shortened, pants hemmed, and waistbands adjusted. It's all part of the clothes-buying adventure.

- You may discover that your body shape requires tops and jackets in Misses sizes and pants in Petite, or vice versa.

- If you have particularly long legs, you may have to shop in Misses departments for pants and skirts and Petites for jackets and tops that proportionally hang at the right spot on your hips and fit a shorter torso.

- By now, you have determined that you have a petite body—meaning that you are relatively short and you are average or somewhere above in weight. This book offers suggestions for all shapes and sizes of the petite body. You may be a different size on top than on the bottom. This is typical, I've found. By now, most suits are sold as separates to ensure a good fit in the jacket and skirt or pants. Two-piece dresses are also sold as separates. Hallelujah!

- Although my clients come in many different shapes and sizes, they all desire the same thing—to look good! To achieve successful results, you must be willing to set aside your old habits of dressing and try new looks, styles, and colors.

- Be patient. You can't do this in one day! Besides trying on clothes at the store, bring home potential winners. In the privacy of your home, you can make better decisions than at the store, where you feel the pressure to buy. Call a friend to come over and help you. She may come up with good questions, comments, and advice.

Petite Departments

Here's a sampling of department stores that have Petite departments:

Ann Taylor	Chadwick's of Boston	J.C. Penney	Marshall Fields	Saks Fifth Avenue
Ann Taylor Loft	Coldwater Creek	J. Jill	Marshalls	Sears
Banana Republic	Dayton's	Kohl's	Mervyns	T.J. Maxx
Bergdorf Goodman	Dillards	Land's End	Meier & Frank	Talbots
Bloomingdales	Eddie Bauer	Lane Bryant	Neiman Marcus	
Bosco's	Fred Meyer	Lord & Taylor	Nordstrom	
Brooks Brothers	J. Crew	Macy's	Robinsons-May	

Petite Departments

Take notes on what you like, and why. Here are a few things to consider:

- First have someone take your body measurements. This will help you and the salesperson choose the right size.

- Does a blouse or knit top minimize your bustline or give you a better shape?

- Does the color of the top bring out your eyes, skin tone, and hair color? If you appear washed out, exchange it for a warmer or cooler color. Which looks best?

- If your hips are large, do the pants fit in a way to minimize your hips, or at least not accentuate your every bump and curve?

- Do the pants have back pockets that maximize or minimize your hips?

- If you're looking for a business pant or a dress pant, the leg should drop easily off your hip and *not* hug your thigh. The same applies to your tummy—not too tight and dropping nicely off the tummy to the upper leg. You'll find that some brands fit your body better than others. Often, inexpensive clothes are cut poorly. Inch yourself up to better-quality stores.

- Well-fitting pants are tough to find. Once you find a manufacturer that matches your body shape, celebrate! Consider buying two or three pairs in your color palette. Manufacturers might change the cut the very next season and you'll be at ground zero—again.

- To learn what is best for you, you have to be willing to try on different styles. When evaluating your body and what looks good or bad, be brutally honest. As you progress, you will find that you can pull fewer clothes and make better decisions—which equals less work and frustration.

- Women who are short often buy jackets that are too long. They dwarf you and make you look dowdy. If you have jackets that are too long but are in good condition, seek out a good alteration person.

- Buying longer jackets to cover a hip problem isn't the solution. Look where the jacket hits, and you'll see what I mean. If your jacket ends 1" or 2" below the fullest part of your hip, the effect should be what you want.

TIP:

When the sleeves of your blouse appear too long, move the cuff button over. Then the sleeve won't fall halfway over your hand—a poor presentation. Putting yourself together properly takes a little time, but it's well worth a minor adjustment or two.

Petite Departments

In front of a
full-length mirror

In front of a full-length mirror

When looking at your figure in the mirror, be honest. And please don't become discouraged. Over the years, I've dressed hundreds and hundreds of women, and I've yet to see Miss Body Perfect.

- Put on a T-shirt. Now look at your neck. Do you have fatty tissue under your chin? Is your neck short or thick? Reach up with a forefinger and pull down the neck of the T-shirt to give the appearance of a V-neck. Is this is a more pleasing look? Showing some skin with an open neck will detract from a short neck and extra skin. This also gives the appearance of more height because you're not all "buttoned up."

- We tend to cover up areas we don't like, but often this *can add to the problem.* With an open neckline, the eye doesn't dwell on the chin but, instead, sees you as taller. Now you're getting the idea of what kind of neckline you should wear. An open neckline might be curved, square, V-neck, or a blouse with collar and lapel laid open. These necklines give the appearance of a person who is open, confident— a more powerful look.

- If your bust is large, you will want to minimize that look. You may have a difficult time finding blouses that close over your bust without pulling sideways. The larger you go up in blouse size, the wider the shoulders will be, so by the time you can button your blouse comfortably, the shoulder seams may be falling off your shoulders. Then the blouse won't feel right—and it isn't.

• Don't panic! Go to the Petite department of several department stores and try on blouses and knit tops. If you find a blouse that fits, is a good color for you, and you'll be able to wear it with several different pants and skirts, buy it. If you can't find any blouses that fit, you might have to go in a slightly different direction. You'll be happier doing this anyway, as you will be looking for *knit tops* that don't button all the way down in front and have a different cut than blouses—*and they stretch.*

Full-Length Mirror

When looking at your figure in the mirror, be honest. And please don't become discouraged.

Tops

Tops

Knit tops

When shopping for knit tops:

- You will have a wide variety to choose from in colors, necklines, and fabrics. To narrow your search, ask yourself: *Is this purchase for casual wear, or do I plan to wear it with a suit or jacket? Is it for evening wear?* Don't just fill your closet with "stuff." Ask yourself: *What am I buying this for, and where do I intend to wear it?* A pretty color, a sale tag, or simply the impulse to buy won't necessarily give you the results you want.

- Knit tops come as flat and ribbed knit, patterned rib, and so on. Buy the knit top that looks best on you, one that minimizes your bustline if needed. Too tight is *not* a good look. Be noticed for the right reasons!

- Knit tops are cut to fit a variety of body shapes, so if you wear a C or D bra size or larger, the side seams of tops should be cut straight down. The sides and the front must have a fuller cut. If a Large or an Extra Large size isn't fitting you in Petite sizes, you will have to go to Misses sizes or to the Plus size Women section. This isn't unusual. The bust will fit, although the top may be a bit longer.

- If the top is too long, have it shortened. Too many women don't buy a garment if it doesn't fit perfectly. With slight alterations, you *can* get a good (nothing is *perfect*) fit. Go for it, gals!

- When buying long- and short-sleeved sweaters, look for the same cuts. The straighter cut on the side seams will give you the fit you need for a larger bust size or extra weight through the middle.

- In selecting fabrics, silk, cotton, wool, linen, cashmere, and blends of these fabrics are best. These are natural fibers. They "breathe," so they will be comfortable in both warm and cool weather. Many knits are mixed with polyester, silk, or rayon, and you'll enjoy those blends, too. The less polyester the better.

- Look at your budget and ask yourself: *How well and for how long do I want these garments to hold up?* Constant washing and drying clothes will wear them down, and soon they will look old and tired. Better-quality clothes hold up longer. Consider hand-washing and flat-drying better knits or machine-washing on the "delicate" cycle, then laying flat or hanging to dry.

TIP: *Silk, cotton, wool, linen cashmere, and blends of these fabrics "breathe," so they will be the most comfortable.*

Knit tops

V-neck, strap:

This is an ideal top to wear under a jacket or cardigan during the day, as the V isn't too deep. In the workplace, you'll want to keep your jacket or cardigan on because the top lends itself more to evening wear.

V-neck, sleeveless:

The V-neckline opens up the neck and face and gives the illusion of height. Slightly fitted side seams, as illustrated, show off a smaller bust. Straighter side seams accommodate a fuller bust.

V-neck, long sleeves:

I like this knit top because of the moder-
ate V trimmed in white and the clever
buckle detail toward the shoulder line.
This top can stand on its own with pants
or a skirt, or it can be worn under
a jacket or cardigan. Notice the fitted
side seams. Try on before buying!

V-neck, 3/4-length sleeves:

Notice the beautiful detail of this top.
If your bust is small to medium, it will
look stunning on you. If you're heavy
in the bust, the detail will accentuate
your breasts. Try it on. If the side seams
are roomy enough, it may work. If you
are really short, the 3/4-length sleeve
will give the illusion of more height.

Knit tops

Round neck, sleeveless:
This basic knit top with a round neckline will be a staple in your wardrobe. If you carry extra weight in your torso, look for tops with a straighter cut in the side seam, to give you a better fit.

Round neck, sleeveless:
Here's a neckline that's slightly curved, and the top has a fuller body cut. This is a good top for the petite lady who needs more room to accommodate a larger bust and weight through the midsection.

Round neck, cap sleeves:

Cap sleeves look good on petites who aren't carrying extra weight in the upper arms. Notice the very basic shape of the neckline. This style invites accessorizing with a necklace or a small, square scarf. (See Accessories.)

Round neck, short sleeves:

This simple, short-sleeved T-shirt is a classic top in 100% cotton. I'd say "no" to wearing it with a good suit or pants, but it will look fine with khakis, jeans, capris, and shorts. Cotton T-shirts are offered in a zillion stores and in many colors. They are cut to fit many different body shapes, so you're sure to find one that will be just right for you.

Knit tops

Round neck with short sleeves:
The vertical lines down the front make the petite lady look taller. And the texture looks equally good with jackets that have a little or a bit more texture. The silk fabric of this savvy top holds its shape and appearance well. It lends itself to necklaces, as well as scarves.

Round neck with 3/4-length sleeves, tight-rib knit:
Petite ladies have to be trim and slim to wear this little number. When you see this top on the hanger, you can tell it's going to be snug-fitting. Often, ample-busted women try to wear this clingy top. The results? The bust spilling out over the top. Not good!

Cutaway neck with short sleeves:
Don't you just love the detail on this top?
But you'll be limited in jacket and cardigan
colors because of the black trim. The top
actually allows a fair amount of room, so
a larger-busted petite woman can wear it.
Women with smaller and medium busts
can wear it, too. It depends on the
fit and style you're looking for.

Cutaway neck with long sleeves:
The washable leather buckle trim shows
what's happening with style in knit tops.
This versatile top can be worn with a
suit or jeans. I'd like to pair it with a
heavier sweater knit in brown or brown
tweed just for the textural difference.
It's an edgy look and adds a unique
style to the wardrobe.

Knit tops

V-neck with tie:

Oh, so soft is the color of this top with the knit string tie. Try different ways of tying the knot—from a square knot to a bow tie. It depends on what looks best on you and what you'll be wearing as a jacket or cardigan.

Round neck with tie:

The different shapes and details of necklines never fail to amaze me! The slightly wider cut in this neckline and the asymmetrical bow make a narrow face appear fuller and narrow shoulders look wider. The cut of the sides allows for varying breast sizes, too.

Semi-square neck with 3/4-length sleeves:

The softly squared neckline with ribbed detail makes narrow shoulders appear wider and fuller. Add a pin or brooch to enhance the effect. The 3/4-length sleeve shows more skin on short women and makes them look taller.

Polo collar neck with 3/4-length sleeves:

Here, a lovely cotton/silk knit is shown in a polo style with 3/4-length sleeves. This knit top can be worn with dress slacks or jeans. Or you can wear it with jeans and a denim jacket or heavier winter-weight jacket.

Knit tops

Square neck with 3/4-length sleeves:
The black knit with ribbed detailing at the neck gives this top a look of distinction. If your face is round or narrow, the neckline diverts attention and balances your face shape. I like the 3/4-length sleeves because the petite woman often has short arms, and when you gently push up the sleeves, the arms look longer.

Wide-banded collar with 3/4-length sleeves:
This stunning knit top with wide-ribbed band collar looks phenomenal on narrow-shouldered women. It gives the illusion of wider shoulders and frames the face. This is a forgiving look for a pear-shaped body, and the extra room at the top allows for larger busts.
A very Marilyn Monroe look!

Mock turtleneck, sleeveless:

Among the favorites in my wardrobe is this silk knit mock turtleneck. I have worn it more times than I can count. It's an off-white basic that subtly goes with and contrasts with many jackets, suits, and cardigan sweaters. If you don't own one, this is a smart buy.

Turtleneck with long sleeves:

If you have a medium to long neck, you can wear a full turtleneck top and not be limited to mock turtles or crewnecks. You will find turtlenecks in many fabrications. The lighter the weight of the fabric, the less bulky it will look.

Blouses

Your "blouse wardrobe" will depend on how often, and where, you wear blouses. Businesswomen pair blouses with suits and also wear them with cardigans or sweater jackets for a casual business look.

Shop for high-quality fabrics. A luscious silk blouse slides on under a suit jacket or a cardigan sweater, and the blouse can stand alone, too. Blouses in 100% cotton look crisp with a skirt or pant. Add a cardigan sweater or jacket and you have a fresh ensemble. Stay away from inexpensive rayon and polyester, as they don't hold up under numerous visits to the drycleaner or the washer and dryer. Sometimes you can find enticing blouses in silk or cotton on sale at the end of the season. Snatch them up for next year!

Button-down short sleeve:
Select a resort-wear floral blouse for the summer months and/or your next warm-climate resort destination. A blouse like this can be found in a variety of fabric blends.

Camp shirts come in colorful florals and prints. Choose one or two that fit your color palette and lifestyle.

Button-down cap sleeve:

This blouse is a true basic and is always in style for the petite woman. You'll appreciate the vertical front tuck pleating, which makes you look taller. A larger-busted lady can wear it by going up in size. For best advantage, you may want a different color next to your face.

Back view:

In the back, you can see the eye-catching detail. A yoke across the shoulder and inverted pleats add to the style—slightly nipped in at the waist but will fit a small to fuller bust by sizing up.

Blouses

Button-down sleeveless:

Because of the sleeveless style, this blouse is ideal for summer. Notice the soft ruffle down the front—so feminine! And the hidden placket hides the buttons. You can wear it under a jacket or a cardigan sweater. The 2½" slit on each side allows you to wear this top over a skirt or flat-front pants or capris. Enjoy!

V-neck sleeveless:

This blouse warms my heart because of the colors in the stripe and the exquisite combined horizontal, vertical, and diagonal stripes. It is cut to fit a small to medium bust. The lovely sheer fabric is lined with pastel fabric, and a side zipper allows for easy on and off. The horizontal stripe comes just under the bust and may not be wide enough to accommodate the larger-busted lady.

Button-down short sleeve:

Lately, more garments are lined or have
a camisole underneath. This way, you
can see and appreciate the sheer fabric
without the garment being inappropriate
in the workplace. The small mandarin
collar with string tie enhances femininity.
The cap sleeves are cut with ample room
and add softness.

Button-down short sleeve:

The black background with a small print
in various colors invites you to wear this
blouse as a jacket by putting a sleeveless
knit top underneath. As you try on
clothes, you'll notice that blouses often
have more than one function. Pair this
one with a black long or short skirt,
pants, or capris.

Blouses

Button-front 3/4-sleeve:
This print blouse is lined except for the sleeves, which are semi-sheer—a nice touch. Blouse treatments vary today, giving buyers the option of wearing them for work or an evening out. The 3/4-sleeve also prevents a too-long sleeve.

Button-front long sleeve:
Your closet will welcome a diagonal, diamond-print blouse in 100% cotton. You can pair it with a work suit or wear it with black slacks on Casual Friday. On the weekend, wear it with jeans or khakis under a sweater.

Button-down long sleeve:

What does it take to perk up and add style to a suit or jacket? This long-sleeved, heavier-weight silk blouse to the rescue. Notice the long cuff, which you can turn under or turn up over the top of your jacket, smart lady!

Button-front long sleeve:

The bias cut of this blouse camouflages either a large or a small bust. It's 100% washable cotton and can partner with jeans in light or dark denim, or black, navy, or white pants. Khaki pants are another good match for this blouse.

Camisoles

Camisoles used to be an under-garment worn to discreetly shield the bra from showing through a sheer garment. Lingerie departments still have camisoles, but the camisoles being designed today are worn in many other ways.

A note of caution: Camisoles are not to be worn alone in a professional business setting—they're too revealing. But you can wear a camisole under a V-neck sweater to shorten the V. Or wear a camisole under a jacket—as long as you don't take the jacket off!

Now for the fun! Wear varying styles and colors with capris, shorts, and jeans. And wear camisoles in the evening, along with a shawl or poncho for style or for warmth.

A simple camisole in a stretch knit and luscious color will go easily with jeans and capris or under a sheer blouse in light pink or the same color. When you pair it with a blouse or top in a different color, the garment takes on a whole new look. Try it!

TIP:

Camisoles can be a terrific new addition to your wardrobe.

This "cami" captured my eye because it has the look of a crocheted garment. It's actually a knit with stretch. Wear it with black jeans or a long, black skirt for evening, enhanced by a black, beaded necklace and earrings.

Both silver and gold jewelry go well with it, too. Keep the jewelry lightweight because the fabric is so delicate. Like many camisoles, this one has a built-in bra.

A turquoise stretch knit with gathers near the bustline helps to give you a good fit. Notice that the cut isn't really low—which gives you a few more options in what kind of lightweight jacket or blouse you can wear with it.

Camisoles

White eyelet always looks fresh and has a bit of sex appeal, too. Eyelet can be worn with jeans, capris, or a tiered white or black skirt. Do you have a lacy cover or shawl to add? You're all set!

This black-and-white print trimmed at the top with white lace and a built-in bra gives you lots of options for day or evening wear. How about a pair of black, medium-weight silk Bermuda shorts or cotton capris? Try different necklaces and earrings for a stylish effect.

ELLEN YORK IMAGE INSTITUTE

TIP:

*Try on different
necklines to see
which look best
with your features.*

Such a pretty stretch knit camisole in green! The design line under the bust and around to the sides adds to the fashion-forward statement.

If you own a tiered skirt in this color or white, you'll look snazzy for a summer evening at the movies or out to dinner with friends.

The shirring detail on the vertical of the bustline will either flatter a full bust or enhance a small bust. How can you lose? And the colors in this lined camisole are so yummy! Wear it with a long or short white silk skirt or wide-legged pants, and strut your stuff.

Jackets

Jackets

Jackets come in all shapes and sizes—as do the lovely ladies who are reading this book. Consider some of the following suggestions.

Jackets for the smaller bust

The following jackets may work for you. Try them on:

- A jacket with collar and lapel.

- A jacket that is no longer than mid-hip or ends just below the fullest part of your hip. Don't go way below the hips, trying to hide them. You'll look short and dumpy instead.

- A jacket without a collar, and with a zipper.

- A jacket with three front buttons. It grows you taller.

- A jacket with darts and design lines. These jackets are slenderizing, show style, and make you appear taller.

Avoid the following jackets:

- Jackets with large patterns, flowers, and plaids. They are overwhelming on petite women.

- Bulky fabrics. They make you feel and look heavier. They also make you look short and boxy—a look you definitely don't want!

This petite jacket can be paired with
either black or winter white pants
and skirts. The beautiful tweed gives
you an idea of the colors you can
choose for blouses and shells
to wear underneath.

Even though the fringe is used
everywhere, it works because
of the softness of the tweed
and quality of the fabric.

A short, simple, understated
necklace would be a good
choice for jewelry.

*Jackets with darts and design lines are slimming and
make you appear taller. Notice the indented sides,
giving your figure more definition.*

Jackets for the smaller bust

The three-button line-up at the front of this jacket will add inches to your height. The small-to-medium bust fits nicely with this design. I like the stylish effect of the slight gathers in the pocket flaps. You'd better not be too hippy to wear this short jacket, though.

The super design of this jacket—with a little more length and a bit more room plus 3/4-length sleeves—will fit a lot of petites. The cuff on the sleeves allows you to show skin, giving the allusion that you're taller. This length is forgiving to women with fuller hips.

If your face is narrow, this collar and lapel will make your face look fuller. The button-tab effect on the pockets is a stylish detail.

Actually, the cut on the sides is more ample than it appears, which allows for some weight you may be carrying through the waist area.

If you're small to medium in the bust and you're a Winter—wow! You're in for a treat! Wear this little silk number with a black skirt (short or long), black pants, or pinstripe slacks. It's a Kristie Burrill design out of Seattle. A short jacket like this compliments petites who don't have a full hip.

Jackets for the fuller bust

If your bust size is 36, 38, or 40, with a C or D cup size or larger, and you're carrying extra weight in the torso, here are some tips:

- Stay away from fitted and more structured styles.

- A jacket with collar and lapels might not suit you, as the eye will be drawn to your bust area and make your breasts appear even more pronounced.

- If a jacket is too tight in the upper arm, move to another jacket style. When you buy clothes that don't fit well, they tend to hang in your closet because they don't feel right or look right when you wear them.

- A dolman or raglan sleeve will diminish fuller arms.

- Try on jackets made of softer fabrics. If they are less structured, they will drape on your body, which will distract the eye from your bust area. You'll start seeing a difference right away.

- There are a lot of feminine looks in jackets for your body type. In addition to drapey fabrics, keep an eye out for necklines that are simple and flattering, like a soft ruffle at the neckline or a slight V-neck.

- Fabrics that are soft are often textured and patterned. Be sure the patterned fabrics are understated so you don't get lost under the jacket.

Notice the room in this jacket, and the simplicity of the design. The soft fabric allows the jacket to drape over the bust area and disguise a full bust. A smaller-busted woman will get lost in this jacket. The 3/4-length sleeves are a boon because you can see the arms—another plus for the petite woman!

I was immediately drawn to this jacket with vertical, quilted stitching. The fabric is lightweight silk—a real advantage to us shorties. The hidden placket hides the zipper closing and keeps the eye moving upward.

- Hold up a jacket and look at the cut. You'll want and need more room in the front for the best fit. If a jacket has darts and curved-fitting seams, chances are you won't have the extra room you'll need. That cut is more for the smaller bust.

- When you're looking at suit jackets, you'll often see skirts (long and short) and pants paired with the jackets. These are generally sold as separates so you can get the fit you need on the top as well as the bottom.

TIP:

Try on jackets made of softer fabrics. If they are less structured, they will drape on your body, which will camouflage your bust area.

The "torn rag" effect of this colorful jacket disguises the large bust. And the array of colors permits you to pair different knit tops underneath—even a camisole.

Unlined, this jacket in an understated print bodes well for the medium to large bust. Because it has no fitting lines or darts, it accommodates extra weight in the upper body. This jacket is not recommended for the tiny, small-busted petite. You'll drown in it!

This 100% silk jacket comes in a variety of colors and can cover a multitude of sins. The 3/4-length sleeves and slits at the side are so appealing. How about leaving the jacket unbuttoned and wearing a shell underneath? Nice!

Outerwear

Everyone needs outerwear of some sort, depending on the climate where you live. Your lifestyle and career will dictate these outerwear garments as well. If your rainy and cold season has some mild days, a lined garment that is water-repellant is a must! If your wardrobe begs for a longer, warmer coat, keep your height and weight in mind as you go shopping. You don't want a coat that takes over your petite size. No fair hiding!

Single-breasted coats and jackets like this one come in water-repellant fabrics. And they are offered in many colors, to give you a lift on dark, rainy days. Many times a zip-out lining is built in so they can be all-weather coats. I like the length of this one—falling just above or just below the knee to keep the petite woman from being overwhelmed by too much coat.

TIP:

Try on any coat before buying. Sometimes you can wear a double-breasted style when the buttons or snaps are small and close together. Or you may prefer the slim, trim look of a single-breasted coat like the one on the opposite page.

This modified trenchcoat in pink offers a welcome relief from black, black, and black. I like the front shoulder flap detail, and the double-breasted front works if the snaps or buttons are placed fairly close together. Style plus a delightful color equals an unbeatable combination.

Outerwear

Let me die over leather! It looks and feels so rich. Some jackets are suede, and others have a smooth finish. Check the gathered pocket detail on this one. Notice the close-fitted design—it appeals to a slim petite. Buy at the end of the winter season and save dollars!

A more forgiving look than the suede style to the left, this fringed jacket hides extra weight and a larger bust. If you're smaller, it works, too, but to carry off the style, be sure you're 5'2" or taller.

Details on leather coats and jackets vary. Fringe and top-stitched seams are common. Leather lasts for years and looks better with age. Pair this jacket with jeans and boots. Or wear it with a tiered lace skirt and cowboy boots. Pizzazz girl!

This jacket is from Carole McClellan, a leather and fur designer in Seattle. Note her choice of lining and button detail.

Cardigans

A lovely sweater set! I'm fond of the cardigan because of the black stitched detail and dark buttons. You can easily see a black blouse or simple black knit top underneath. The style is good for petites because the back length is only 23"!

This cardigan in a stunning color and updated style will take your breath away. The subtle, understated, print design will bring you raves. And, as a bonus, it's slenderizing. Don't you love the soft ruffle on the sleeve? Wear this cardigan with navy pants, skirt, or jeans.

Color on color is a good look. But imagine interchanging different-colored cardigan and top combinations you may already have. A little ingenuity makes good use of new purchases, too. No guilt here! A 25½" back-length accommodates a larger hip.

A short cardigan with clever eyelet detail looks stylish with a knit top in the same color or other colors under it. This combination is ideal for the short, petite lady—best worn by ladies with smaller hips.

Cardigans come in many styles and fabrications. Have fun with your choices.

Sweater jackets

Everyone should own one or two sweater jackets, especially if you live in a chilly climate or work in a building where you shiver in the air-conditioning. The styles are becoming so contemporary and practical! Most zip up the front, and they're roomier than a regular cardigan, allowing you to wear a blouse or a pullover sweater underneath.

Be sure the sweater jacket blends nicely into your wardrobe. Wear this versatile garment with short and long straight skirts, khakis, dress pants, and jeans.

You'll find sweater jackets in plain colors as well as patterns. Stay away from heavy garments that add too much bulk to your short body. The selection is plentiful, so you'll find something that looks just right on you!

Here's a sweater jacket in brown and black tweed with a contemporary look. The sweet pinky-coral trim sets it off nicely. You can wear this one with a brown shell or a turtleneck. Even black goes with it.

The body of the sweater is short and angular—flattering to the petite lady. Short and long straight skirts, as well as dress pants, make an ideal combination, and brown or black cords and jeans are fine, too.

ELLEN YORK IMAGE INSTITUTE

I envision you at the ski lodge or cuddling in front of a fireplace in this hand-knit sweater jacket. It goes with ski pants, jeans, or a nice dress slack. Couple the look with boots for real style.

The Icelander sweater is always a popular choice, and the multitude of colors in this one give you many choices in pants and skirts. Mock turtles and turtlenecks, as well as blouses, all can be worn underneath.

These tried-and-true garments will become staples in your wardrobe for years to come.

Sweater jackets

This tweed sweater is a good choice for Casual Fridays at work, and it's a fine match for the petite woman's body. A mock turtleneck looks good underneath—or a basic blouse in navy or white with a collar and lapel. Wear this sweater with khaki pants, jeans, or wool pants.

Soft as cashmere—only this one is a wool/nylon blend that zips up the front. If you're carrying a lot of extra weight, you'd better not buy it. The trim petite will wear this style best.

ELLEN YORK IMAGE INSTITUTE

TIP:

Look for sweaters in different textures, but make sure they are lightweight, not heavy and bulky. That's too much for your short body!

The collar style in a new rib width gives this light blue number a fresh look. The price is just right, too. You know you'll wear it a lot, so go ahead and buy it! Notice the length— ideal for the petite gal. If you have a medium to large bust, simply go up in size.

Sweaters and sweater sets are often good alternatives to jackets, and they have become extremely popular.

Pants

Pants

Pants are probably the toughest item to find for your body, my body, and the bodies of the vast majority of women. I've worked with many designers, trying to explain what women really need for pants to fit, and gradually pants are starting to fit the real human body!

For the hard-to-fit woman, pants have to be cut with some or all of the following:

- Room across the front
- Room in the hip area
- Extra room in the waist
- Extra room in the thigh
- A longer or shorter crotch seam
- A flat-front design cut with more room versus pleats.

Of course, we aren't all built the same, so our needs are different. That's where the challenges begin. Notice that all three pairs of pants shown here are a flat-front design—a more flattering cut than pleats, which add bulk to your body shape. Petites—we don't need that, do we?

Brown pants are a must for nearly every wardrobe. This pair drops just below the waist. If your waist is larger than normal like mine, the drop waist will give you a good fit because the top is cut with more room. Voila! I walk out of the store with pants that fit!

Pants

Pants come in many different styles, cuts, and leg shapes. You will have to allot some serious dressing-room time to find the right style for your body shape. Take a pair of heels with you to get a better idea of how the pants will look.

You may wear an off-white pant from April through September. This stylish pant is cut with a wide leg that drops gracefully off the hip. Dress pants shouldn't cling to every curve of your body. They aren't cut like jeans, so please don't try for that kind of fit.

Charcoal gray is a good choice for many petites who already own one or two pairs of black slacks. The pant shown here has the bonus of being stretch wool, which feels good next to the skin. The leg is straighter and can be worn with heels or ankle boots in black.

Slacks

Pants in a pinstripe go with many garments you'll see in this book. Notice that these have a wider leg with a slight flair at the bottom. This is a good style to wear if you're a bit hippy and/or you have a larger bust. The total look is balanced and well-proportioned.

Wear pinstripes as a way to look taller and slimmer. The fabric borrows from men's suits.

- If you're buying pants for the workplace, church, and dressier occasions, you'll want a better-quality fabric—silk, wool, polyester/wool and rayon/wool. Many pants are made with a percentage of Lycra. So much the better. They feel good, and the Lycra allows the fabric to stretch both ways across the tummy, hips, and legs. Nowadays, many dress pants, as well as casual pants, are made with stretch fabric. How many years have we had stretch fabric in swimsuits? Bring it on, retailers! We're ready for comfort.

- Buy pants for your body shape. Some pants have pleats in the front, and others have flat fronts (no pleats, or just one pleat). With front pleats, the leg is cut with more room. When you stand in front of the mirror, you may think there's too much fabric in the leg. Some manufacturers cut a flat front and a pleated front in the same fabric and colors. Try both to see which looks best on you in the same color and fabric.

- If you have a tummy problem, flat-front pants are more flattering. Find a pair that's cut with enough room in the front. If the pants are too tight across the front, the pleats produce "drag lines"—they pull sideways—and add to the poor fit.

- Companies and businesses are in constant turmoil regarding dress-down or Casual Fridays. The answer is for them to specify exact rules in their dress code. Read and adhere to your company's dress policy.

I'll bet most petites reading this book will look best in flat-front pants.

Jeans

TIP:

Many shoe and boot styles can be worn with jeans. A boot-cut jean allows you to wear high heels if you want, too!

- Jeans come in as many styles and proportions as you can imagine and sometimes occupy an entire department in themselves. To narrow the search, first consider your age. If you're 35 years old, don't frustrate yourself trying to shop in the Junior department, where jeans generally are cut shorter in the crotch, slimmer in the leg, and smaller in the waist and hip. As we age, our proportions change, so you must change your brands, as well as the style you buy and the departments you visit.

- My number-one pet peeve is to see women wearing pants with a short rise that reveals their belly button. Soooo tacky! And consider the bulge of skin in this area—not for public viewing. When you bend over to pick up something, your underwear shows and—worse—the crack in your bottom is exposed.

- If you're looking for an attractive pair of casual pants or khakis, visit a well-stocked Petite department. Your challenge will be to take the time to find a style and size that will fit you as well as possible. When you do find "that perfect fit"—and you will, if you persevere—buy two or three pairs. The manufacturer might change the cut next season.

- Take four or five pairs of different styles and sizes into the dressing room. Then you'll have a chance to see and compare what they look like on your body and you won't have to get dressed and go searching the floor again.

- If you're a petite with long legs, you will undoubtedly shop in Misses sizes, not Petite departments.

Have fun with belts—be different, and be stylish.

Pants

Suits

Suits

When your lifestyle requires you to wear a suit daily or for certain occasions, the selection has never been more plentiful. Those of you who aren't actively involved in a career still may want to wear a suit for meetings and events that require business attire. You may be on a board of an organization or participate with business people in other settings where you want to fit in.

Suits today are much prettier and more feminine than they used to be. If you have occasions to wear suits—work or otherwise—buy and enjoy. Take a look at those pictured here. You'll see a lot of variety—and they're flattering, too.

Wool crepe is still a basic fabric for suits and looks outstanding in different colors. You can wear this short jacket if you're not hippy. If you're carrying weight in the hips, go for a longer jacket like the ones you see to the right.

Here's a slimming style. It has medium lapels, and the two-button closing is placed where it gives you more height. The pants are cut fuller, which camouflages either skinny or fuller legs. The plain color allows you plenty of choices in knit tops and blouses. Be careful that the blouse you choose isn't too casual for the suit fabric. When in doubt, seek the advice of a salesperson or a trusted friend.

This pinstripe suit works with a variety of body shapes. If you're larger in the bust and generally heavy in the torso, you'll do well with this style. The roomy legs flatter the petite woman with heavier hips and thighs. This suit is also flattering on a slim, trim gal. The slight flair of the pants helps to balance the hip and bust.

Suits

- Whatever the occasion, refer to your color palette and purchase one or more suits that show off your best colors.

- For the petite woman, your suit jackets, pants, and skirts are cut proportionally for your shorter frame. Most jackets you see in Petites are shorter for a good reason: A jacket that is too long dwarfs the petite woman. (Remember—you always want to appear taller.)

- Because our body shapes are all different, we require different sizing. My suit jackets are Misses size 6, and my pants and skirts are often a Petite 6.

TIP:

Many times, our size depends on our exercise program. Yes, exercising can change our proportions!

This is a basic suit cut, but notice the yoke at the shoulder piped in pink and duplicated in a diagonal piece at the hem—a nice touch! The various colors in the fabric allow you ample color choices for blouses and knit tops to wear with this suit.

In a fabric that's more than a pinstripe, you can show off this suit with a light blue, light tan, or taupe blouse or knit top—or an off-white silk blouse or knit shell. The three-button jacket will make you look taller, too. The jacket is a bit longer than I usually recommend but still fine for the petite woman 5'2" to 5'4". If you're under 5'2", wear a shorter jacket or have an alterations person shorten it.

Here's a smart and edgy brown tweed suit with zipper detail in the skirt and sleeve. The suit is completely reversible to brown. Wear it with brown opaque hose and heels or boots. When you reverse to the brown side, have fun with tops in various colors. How about a brown and off-white striped knit top? Mmmm. . . .

Suits

There's a suit style for everyone!

- Many suit pieces are sold as separates. This allows you the best fit possible.

- Suits that used to be boring now have a bit of an edge. It's much more fun to get dressed in the morning!

TIP:

Notice the different ways to put this suit together. It also lends itself to a silk blouse with collar and lapels in white, off-white, pink, mauve, or light blue.

Here's a flattering suit for petites, a medium-weight wool in deep burgundy. The skirt is cut on the bias—so flattering on any body. And notice the sheer chiffon trim at the hemline of the skirt.

You may appear at a luncheon or business dinner dressed in the understated elegance of a camisole under the suit. The softness of a silk camisole enhances the evening look, too.

A mauve cashmere top with a sprinkling of sparkles will show off your good taste in clothes. Don the suit jacket and leave the buttons undone so people can see the lovely top. A pair of black heels is the right finishing touch.

Mixing and matching suit pieces

When you're looking for suits, I hope you'll find one or two that you'll be able to mix and match in some way with clothes you already own. You'll end up with a wardrobe that gives you more mileage.

Sometimes a suit is sold as a two-piece outfit and you can't buy just one piece or the other. Don't fret. This may open your eyes to clothes you have in your closet that will blend with one or both pieces of your new two-piece suit.

For instance, you may feel confident in purchasing a pretty white jacket assembled with a black skirt (sold as a two-piece suit) because you own a pair of black pants and another style of black skirt to wear with it. You can work the white jacket through your wardrobe with various tops, skirts, and pants. The jacket may be the answer to a dress you have that's crying for a jacket!

Tops and blouses that will go well with your new suit may be in different colors, in keeping with your color palette, of course. Red, pink, yellow, fuchsia, black and white stripes, or plain black—all are color ideas that might show off your two-piece suit to advantage.

Don't forget a simple necklace or a small, square scarf as accessories. And how about earrings that match or go with the necklace or scarf? A brooch you found in a thrift store or an estate sale will look nifty on the lapel of the jacket.

Whether you choose to wear a skirt or pants is up to you. I like to have some of each so I don't get bored with my wardrobe.

The green blouse and pants together dictate your choice in jacket color to round out the total look. Consider a jacket in black, white, camel, brown, or a pinstripe.

Here's the pinstripe jacket in a mushroom brown with a stripe that matches the green. Notice the jacket length—just right for the petite lady. If you're not hippy, go for a jacket 2½" longer

TIP:

As you bring home new clothes, look through your closet for other blouses, knit tops, and jackets that will complement your new duds.

This mushroom-brown lined silk pant lends itself to tops in lime green, coral, pink, or the same shade of brown. The same color of jacket in the same fabric also would be effective with a multi-stripe blouse or knit top, or a small-print blouse. For shoes, select brown pumps or boots.

When you add a pinstripe jacket to the pants, the outfit takes on a whole new look. Try a print or striped knit top for a gently edgy look. Be willing to experiment. It will take extra time, and perhaps visiting several stores, to achieve just the look you want. But what you end up with is what will make it you, you, you!

TIP:

Whenever the top matches the pant or skirt, you have options in jacket color. It's also a very slimming look.

Suits

Black pants and a black knit top invite a wide variety of jacket color options to complete the total look. Turquoise, burnt orange, black tweed, cobalt blue, purple—it's your call.

This jacket was shown in the store as part of an ensemble. It works here, too, with black pants—and in a number of different combinations. If you already own black pants and blouses or tops, you'll be surprised at how well you can mix and match. Hey, you're on your way to a more interesting wardrobe.

Skirts

Skirts

The subject of skirts is much easier to explore than the topic of pants because we've eliminated the crotch and the entire problem it can present. Skirts are smart and snappy—and your walk changes when you're wearing them. You move with ease because you're not thinking about the way you look, as you do in pants. Skirts are more forgiving of your body shape, too. You simply have to hem the skirt at the most flattering place on your legs.

A short, straight skirt like this one is a *must* in your closet. It should be a color that will mix and match with many tops and jackets. The skirt length should be 1 – 2" above the knee, mid-knee, or no longer than just below the knee.

TIP:

All legs have good and bad places to set a hem. Find the most flattering length for you.

A basic black skirt with a bias-cut drape will carry you to many day and evening functions. The tops and shoes you wear will define where you'll be wearing this skirt. The elastic at the waist will give you hours of comfort.

A long, straight skirt in a basic color is an essential piece of clothing in your closet. Try on this style to see if it's right for your body shape and height. To make the long skirt work, you'll need 2" heels in boots or shoes, and a jacket no longer than mid-hip. The boots should have a pointed toe and no wide, clunky heels, please!

- When purchasing skirts, ask yourself where and for what occasion you will be wearing them. This will lead you to the appropriate fabric and style.

- For the workplace, I take some of my clients from business pants into several different skirt shapes, depending on the size and length of their legs.

- If you're purchasing a straight skirt for the office, please don't get one with a hem any shorter than 2" above the knee! Otherwise, when you sit down, the skirt will hike up your legs. This clearly is not appropriate for the office, yet many women are guilty as charged on this matter!

- Have the alterations person pin the skirt at several different lengths. All legs have good and less than good places to set a hem. Find the most flattering length for each skirt you buy.

An "A"-line skirt can be so flattering to the petite woman. Skirts like this one hide larger hips and heavier thighs and also look good on slim petites. I like the pink piping that separates the skirt from the bias cut 4" at the base of this skirt.

This bias-cut skirt with fringe at the hem has a flattering drape. Be creative and pair it with a variety of solid-colored tops. Try different jackets, to create different looks you may want for your lifestyle.

This summer skirt with cocoa background adorned with pink flowers will look sweet with a pink knit top and a brown cardigan sweater. The skirt has an easy, feminine "swing."

Skirts

Skirts are smart and snappy. You move with ease because you're not thinking about the way you look in pants.

- Try on a longer skirt with a softer cut. Mark the hem at the most flattering place on your calf. If your ankles are thin, set the hem 3" to 4" shorter to show a fuller part of your leg.

- A drapey skirt worn with a jacket or cardigan sweater can look professional and feminine at the same time. This look masks hip and tummy problems and also hides heavy thighs, which are more pronounced with pants.

- Softer skirts come in many different cuts. Look for a style that is slenderizing and makes you look taller.

- You will find skirts in a wide array of floral patterns, prints, and plain colors. Fabrics may be poly/rayon, silk, soft cotton, or drapey rayon. If you have good legs, here's your chance to shine. And the selection of smart, wearable skirts *gets better with each new season.*

Softness in skirts is more popular than ever and hides a multitude of bumps and bulges around the waist, hips, and thighs. The elastic waist spells c-o-m-f-o-r-t. A new twist is the sheer detail at the hemline—the height of fashion.

TIP:

A bias-cut skirt has a beautiful drape, falling smoothly over your body.

Don't you just love a bias-cut skirt? The diagonal cut results in a soft, flowing drape. When you combine this skirt with an off-white silk blouse with a bit of ruffle at the neckline, you'll look totally feminine.

The cut of this skirt is fuller. Try it on. The fabric is so lightweight that you might be surprised at how good you look in it. Combine it with tops in colors you find in the skirt. A black jacket will round out the total look.

You will find gently flowing skirts in a wide array of floral patterns, prints, and plain colors.

Dresses

Dresses

Great dresses are often hard to find, but with a little patience and trying some on, you can spot a winner. The amazing thing is that a dress may look awful on the hanger and awesome on your body, and vice versa. So try on, try on, and try on some more.

- If a one-piece dress for the office, church, or a special occasion is difficult to find, look for a two-piece dress (a skirt with a matching top). These two pieces then can be mixed and matched throughout your wardrobe.

- When your two-piece dress has a buttoned blouse, use it like a jacket and put a complementary shell underneath. Another plus for the two-piece dress!

- Sleeveless dresses require a jacket or cardigan sweater in the workplace. If the sleeveless dress can be dressed up enough for the theater, symphony, or opera, wear a pretty shawl, a dressy poncho, or a beaded cardigan sweater.

- When you're shopping for a shawl, poncho, or jacket, take the dress with you, to match or complement colors and fabrics.

Sometimes the best and quickest answer is a two-piece dress—a skirt with a matching blouse.

What's more versatile than a two-piece dress? Look where you can go with tops to wear under this one! I like this dress with just the blouse and skirt...plus navy pumps or a strappy shoe.

The same skirt is accented here with a fuchsia knit top and a navy cardigan. Could the top still be a plain color but without trim? Absolutely!

- I'm always thrilled when I find a dress that has a good accompanying jacket. Still, consider jackets and wraps you might already own to wear with the new dresses you buy.

- You are a Petite size whether you are size 4 or 16. So look for dress styles that will be the most flattering on *you*. If you're carrying extra weight under your breasts and through the tummy area, an empire waist will help disguise that part of your body.

- Knit dresses with style lines and seams can show off your body shape to your best advantage. Wool, cotton, and jersey knits are all possibilities. When you spot a fabulous dress—buy it. These dresses blow out of a store quickly, so don't wait for them to go on sale. They won't be there by then.

TIP:

The print or stripe in the fabric tells you what other colors you can wear in blouses, knit tops—even shoes!

Just look at the bias-cut top on this dress! That alone covers a multitude of curves and weight problems. The top hides either a very small or a large bust. The skirt is styled for Petite sizes 4 through 16. Wear it with a cardigan or jacket in black or various shades of brown. Shoes in black or brown will complement this nifty dress.

This paisley print in hues of blue is made for the Summer lady. The soft drape of the skirt enhances the petite figure. To turn the blouse into a jacket, wear a light blue or off-white shell under it.

Shoes to complement the dress may be navy or off-white. And try a navy or off-white cardigan or jacket to top it off.

For the Autumn woman, this two-piece dress will be a hit. Notice the drape of the skirt—so forgiving on your body. The myriad of colors will enable you to pick jackets and cardigans in any of the colors to toss on top. You can wear the top as a sleeveless jacket and choose one of the colors for a sleeveless knit top to wear under it.

Give your wardrobe a lift with a basic dress. You'll be able to accessorize it in many different ways for occasions from casual to dressy. If scarves aren't for you, how about a one-, two-, or three-strand pearl necklace?

TIP:

For petite women, the hemline shouldn't fall below mid-knee and should look good on your frame.

Here's a dress in a linen and rayon blend. The rayon keeps the dress from wrinkling. The dress is also fully lined—which means you don't have to wear a slip.

Style lines and seams can show off your body shape to your best advantage.

TIP:

If you don't have a neck (to speak of), avoid scarves like the plague!

How you accessorize is up to you and the image you want to project. If a belt flatters your waistline, purchase a 3/4" to 1½" belt. A small, square scarf may suit you more than the oblong shape. Here's your chance to radiate a new style!

Look in your closet. You may already own a jacket that will complement the dress. No belt? No scarf? A simple strand of pearls or a beaded necklace would be fine.

A sleek sheath dress flatters the petite lady. Larger sizes will allow room in the torso for a medium to large bust. Be inventive with scarves and brooches that pick up or contrast nicely with the color of the dress.

Versatile is the name of the game when you purchase this jacket. It's made to go with the sheath dress but may be worn with other dresses, pants, or skirts you have already.

You're fortunate when you find a basic dress with a knee-length jacket to accompany it. Wear a pearl or silver necklace and an attractive brooch on the jacket lapel. This attractive ensemble will take you many places. The empire waist will cover a multitude of sins, too!

TIP:

Consider jackets and wraps you might already have to wear with the new dresses you buy.

When you find a basic black, navy, or brown dress like this one in two-way stretch fabric, buy it! You can wear this two-piece number all day and into the evening. To change the look, put on a jacket or cardigan and accessorize with earrings and a wrap to suit the occasion.

This dress stands out because of the various colors that invite accessorizing. The design is basic, but the ruffle at the sleeve hem tells you it's *now!* Visualize the finished look: a small, square scarf, tied asymmetrically at the neck, in a plain color of orange, pink or gold—with earrings to match. Wear it out to lunch or to the office.

ELLEN YORK IMAGE INSTITUTE

TIP:

Take three or four dresses into a dressing room at once to avoid frustration and wasted time.

Aren't you wild about all the color in this dress! Immediately you start visualizing cardigans and jackets that will look stunning with it. Think white, black, off-white, watermelon. This is a worthy look for the office. Or top it with a shawl and you're set for an evening occasion.

Please yourself with an asymmetrical wrap dress. The 3/4-length sleeve can be pushed up slightly and you're off to work, a day of shopping, or meeting friends for dinner.

With this dress, I'd suggest limiting your accessories to earrings only.

Evening wear

Evening wear

Two-piece dressing is an answer to putting together your after-five wardrobe. Well-stocked Petite departments often have a dressier section. If they're all mixed in together, ask a salesperson for help.

- Find the skirt or pant first. You'll be carrying around fewer clothes while you try to find tops. Often your best bet, and only choice, is black in pants and skirts, hopefully in several styles and skirt lengths.

- With pants or skirt draped on your arm, go looking for evening-wear tops. They come in a variety of fabrics including silk, silk/rayon, two-way stretch, and silk/poly blends. If you're carrying extra weight through your torso, make sure the top doesn't cling to your body.

- In larger cities and larger stores the selection will be better. Also, many boutiques have a good selection of evening pieces. As the holidays come around, the selection will be even better.

- The fabric is different from daytime wear. It's dressier. You'll see textured fabrics and subtle prints. Think stretch velvet and other stretch fabrics in tops, pants, and skirts. Silk skirts, if available, have a drape that is pure heaven.

- Texture means black-on-black, or a subtle print in black—maybe leaves, flowers, or an understated pattern. White and other colors are referred to in the same manner as white-on-white, navy-on-navy, turquoise-on-turquoise, and so on.

A shawl is one way to enhance evening wear.
You'll be surprised to find pieces in your current wardrobe
that will enhance the new pieces that you bring home.

- Evening skirt styles for petites won't be voluminous. They can be long, slightly gathered, or gored. Don't forget bias cuts.

- With evening wear, you can shine and show off your personality with color, sequins, beading, jewelry, and sparkly shoes.

- Consider gored skirts that aren't real full, and skirts with flounces or ruffles at the hem, in various lengths. Take a variety into the dressing room to get an idea of the style that's best for you.

- What's amazing and surprising is how different a garment can look on the hanger and on you. When you put it on, it takes on a life of its own. Good and not-so-good surprises await you! But you'll never know 'til you try on a few pieces.

- At all times, evening wear should accomplish the same results that your other clothes do. It should flatter, be comfortable, and fit your body type.

- If you're looking for an ankle-length straight skirt, your choices may be black, black, or black. But the good news is that it may be stretch fabric with an elastic waist. (The elastic will be sewn to the top layer of the skirt, rolled over once or twice, and tacked down on the sides, front, and back.) The skirt then will be a pull-on skirt with a long slit or back pleat, or perhaps a side slit.

- A skirt drapes over your hips, tummy, and legs, eliminating the difficulty in trying to find evening pants that fit. Once you eliminate the crotch seam, you're halfway home!

With evening wear, you can show off your personality through your choices in jewelry, evening wraps, and shoes. This two-piece dress, off-white shawl, earrings, necklace, and strappy shoes accompanied me to a New York Broadway show!

- Softly patterned and print pants and skirts should be styled and cut for evening wear. Again, take several pieces into the dressing room. If you decide on one, head out to look for an appropriate evening top to go with it. Keep in mind that your color and pattern are now in the skirts or pants, so the top should be simple and elegant. Think satin for tops and jackets, or satin or silk for a shell top and velvet for the jacket. Also think shawls.

- The sleeve length for your top will depend on what kind of jacket or wrap (poncho, shawl, or decorative cardigan sweater) you own or are intending to buy. You'll see sleeveless, short-sleeved, 3/4-length, and long sleeves. Pick a top that complements the skirt, in color, texture, fabric, and design.

You'll turn heads in this floral dress in a two-way stretch fabric. You should be 5'3" – 5'4" to carry off the large print. The design with gathers coming off the center front allows for a bust size from small to large. Wear this dress with strappy evening shoes, a colorful shawl, and drop earrings.

TIP:

A shawl goes well with any sleeve length.

With this nifty dress, you can play with accessories and wear it to many different events. It's floaty and fun, and you'll wear it for many years to come. The softness of the cut can hide a multitude of sins, and the uneven hem beckons the short woman to wear it with confidence.

Win raves when you wear this little black dress with a splash of glitter. Softness in the sleeves adds to the elegance. Go up in size and you'll artfully disguise your bust and hipline. For a more dramatic look, bring out your diamonds, pearls, rhinestones, and beaded jewelry.

Evening wear

- Ask a salesperson for help with your final decision, or take your favorites home and ask your best "clothes friend" for advice. If you ask your teenage children for advice, remember that they're younger and view the fashion world through their peers' eyes—which often relate more to "in" brand names than what looks good on an individual body.

- Expect a lot of glitter, but seek what looks best on you.

- Perhaps you already own some tops and jackets in evening-wear fabrics. Keep in mind that velvet is reserved for late fall and winter seasons, not for spring and summer events.

Try on this little number before you rule it out. It's so delicate with three tiers of silk fabric. If you've gained 20 – 30 pounds, this dress will camouflage the extra weight. And if you're strikingly trim, you'll look stunning.

The dress speaks for itself, so don't overdo the accessories. Earrings and a sparkly comb in your hair will be enough. You may prefer a slingback pump instead of a strappy shoe. Your choice!

TIP:

Evening wear is all over the board. Zero-in by asking yourself: What's my social life? How dressy is it? How often do I go out? Answers to these questions will help you shop smarter.

I've owned this shawl for five years and I couldn't count the number of times I've worn it. A good shawl can do that for you, so try on other tops you own and see if you can get more mileage out of it. The softness of black stretch pants is ideal for evening wear. Another idea? A sparkly stretch pant as shown.

- Sometimes a jeweled, off-white, black, green, or red cardigan sweater will blend beautifully with your newfound skirt or pants.

- If you want or already own a sequined jacket, keep your skirt or pants and top simple so your "main show" is the jacket.

- Don't over-accessorize if the color and decoration in the fabric is enough. A pair of earrings, a classy ring, and perhaps a bracelet will be sufficient.

- Take time to try things on long before the event you are planning to attend. Then you can choose just the right ensemble to feel and look on top of the world.

If your skirt and top are taking you to a wedding, here are some important things to know:

- What time of day or evening will the wedding be?

- Where will the wedding be held—inside or outside?

- Where will the reception be?

- If the wedding is a big event, you will have more options to put some pizzazz in your dressing.

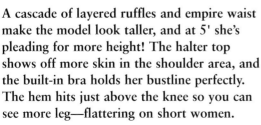

TIP:

Keep your options open. Neither of these dresses was in the Petite department. I simply looked for a short dress in a size 2.

A cascade of layered ruffles and empire waist make the model look taller, and at 5' she's pleading for more height! The halter top shows off more skin in the shoulder area, and the built-in bra holds her bustline perfectly. The hem hits just above the knee so you can see more leg—flattering on short women.

Because she looks so good in a halter dress, here's that look again—but in a different dress style. The cut of the dress shows off her dainty features, and with her slim body, she can wear the fullness in the bottom of the dress. The flower and ribbon detail, plus the sheer hem, convey personal style.

The basic black dress— goes day into evening

When you find a two-piece dress, open your mind to the many possibilities of where you can wear it and the many ways you'll be able to accessorize it.

A long, oblong, silk scarf can be transported below the waist as a sash. And think of the endless possibilities for shoes!

*One dress like this
in your closet will give
you many options.*

For daytime, consider a scarf at the neck. You don't like scarves? Necklaces to the rescue. They don't add bulk at your neckline and around your face.

You can wear this dress to the office. Going out after work? Put jewelry, shawl, and evening shoes in a bag for an easy change after work.

Evening wrap options

You'll look demure in this sequined bolero. Underneath, you might wear a camisole in white, black, or light pink satin. If it cuts you in half and makes you look shorter, don't buy it!

Often in our evenings out, we attend small gatherings for cocktails and dinner. This evening cardigan, adorned with pearls and sequins, offers a relaxed, less dressy look.

Wear this off-white, trimmed-in-gold wrap to set off silky black or gold pants or a long skirt. The gold lamé mock turtle is beautiful underneath. Try some camisoles, too. Now you're all set for an enjoyable evening on the town.

This generously sparkled, sheer jacket stops just above the knee. It radiates elegance when worn with a basic black dress or a black shell and black pants. Awesome!

Clothing for
Plus-size petites

Clothing for Plus-size petites

Petite cuts are necessary to fit women 5'4" and shorter. When clothing in the Petite department doesn't fit, go to the Plus-size department and have the salesperson show you where the Petite sizes are. They're marked with the size, followed or preceded by "P" for Petite—14P, 22P, and so on. In regular Petite departments, the sizes typically run from 0 through 14 or 16, sometimes 18. In Plus-size departments, Petites often are mixed with regular Plus sizes. The salesperson will be able to guide you.

The 3/4-length sleeves and slightly wider neckline are creatively timmed in black. The knit top is shorter to accommodate the short petite woman. These flat-front pants are slenderizing, yet allow room for extra weight in the thigh, hip, and tummy.

Don't be surprised to find Misses sizes that fit in tops and dresses.

The soft version of power dressing

A sweater set is a natural accompaniment to pinstripe pants. Here, a pink cardigan with matching pink top provides a complete look. And how nice it looks when you substitute black pants or skirt!

How far can one pair of pants go? A long way when coordinated with complementary tops. Here, the black cardigan with pink trim and removable flower are a good match for the pants and stripe. A simple black shell goes underneath.

- Many times you're between regular Petite sizes but must go to Petite Plus to get a better fit, depending on where you're carrying your weight. This is common, especially if you're on a weight-loss program or you've suddenly gained weight. Work between the two departments until you're satisfied with the look and fit.

- Spend time in these departments. Ask questions. You will find everything from capri pants and T-shirts to suits, jackets, blouses, dresses, skirts, and casual and dress pants. While you're browsing in the Plus sizes, you may discover that certain manufacturers offer tops and blouses that fit you. You may have to shorten them a bit, but the basic fit is there.

- Manufacturers and designers cut large women's Petite sizes with the same idea as Petite women's sizes 0 through 16. They allow for extra weight and room in the torso, arms, hips, tummy, and legs. The crotch will be shorter, and pants, tops, blouses, and jackets will be shorter, too.

A multi-stripe jacket allows you to wear a wide variety of different-colored T-shirts and blouses underneath. This jacket can be worn with jeans, khakis, or a relaxed knit pant.

TIP:

If you're not pleased with your look in shorts, let the capri pant be your answer to summer and vacation clothing.

How many colored T-shirts do you own that would look nice with these pink capri pants? The Petite Plus woman will find T-shirts that are cut wide with extra room in the bust and tummy area if that's what you need.

A popular resort print is shown here in a camp shirt style. These prints are offered in an interesting assortment of patterns and color schemes. The capri pants are available in many colors and styles, too. Enjoy your shopping spree!

In the late 1980s, as I was about to make the transition from the dress design business to an Image Consulting career, a man approached me wanting me to design and manufacture a line of clothing for the Plus-size woman. One of the biggest mistakes I ever made was to say "no." Clothing for big gals has become a tremendous business today, and the improvements are exciting. Today's selections offer more color, better designs, and improved fabrications for all shapes and sizes.

You'll readily find blouses and tops to wear with your black pants. Because of the sheer fabric, this blouse requires a camisole, so don't forget to stop by the lingerie department. Many tops come with built-in camisoles or are partially lined.

Here's a chic dress in polka dots for day or after-five. The slenderizing cut flows gently over the bust, hips, and thighs. The graceful V-neck and short, ruffled sleeves convey *feminine* for the Plus-size petite woman.

For daytime, wear this dress with a black or lime green cardigan or jacket. For evening, top it with a shawl.

A new designer attitude says okay to ruffles at the neck and sleeve. Such a lady-like look! The cut of this blouse camouflages all the areas you don't want to show off. Better looking clothes for the bigger gals? Yes, indeed!

Today, designers are stepping up their efforts for Plus-size women—in design, fabrics, and fit. You'll be surprised, and pleased, at the wide selection and array of garments from which to choose.

Well-fitting pants in Petite sizes are essential for the Plus gal. It surely beats rolling the waistband several times to get a pant to fit, doesn't it? As you've found out by now, skirts are less demanding because you don't have the crotch to deal with.

The crinkled fabric of this blouse provides a nice contrast to the classic black pants. The blouse comes with a camisole to offset its sheerness. The blouse can be worn with skirts and jeans, too.

Clothing for the larger woman is a tremendous business today, with vast improvements in color and style.

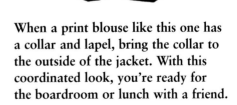

TIP:

Give yourself enough time to shop and try on a variety of garments. Often, when a top is offered only in Misses sizes, your remaining challenge will be simply to have it shortened.

Whether you're a career gal or want to pull together a wardrobe that enhances your lifestyle, a jacket like this one in turquoise will become essential to your wardrobe.

When a print blouse like this one has a collar and lapel, bring the collar to the outside of the jacket. With this coordinated look, you're ready for the boardroom or lunch with a friend.

If you're ready for something new and different, try this subtle animal print in sheer fabric. You can wear any number of shells or camisoles under it. Pair this spicy blouse with pants, skirts, even jeans, and get adventuresome with shoes, too.

You'll look breathtaking in the ruffles of this feminine blouse. The stylish seam under the breasts will accommodate your figure very well, and the not-too-low-V-neck is fine for the office with a cardigan or jacket.

Plus-Size Petites

This two-piece black dress has exquisite embroidered trim at the neckline and hem of the skirt. Be creative—perhaps turquoise earrings and necklace.
To complete the look, wear Western boots—no kidding!—or an up-do-date strappy wedge shoe.

In this luscious empire top, notice how the fabric drops from the curved seamline. This elegant garment is guaranteed to fit the Plus-size petite without being too tight. Wear it with capris, jeans, or khakis.

Figure challenges

Figure challenges

The Challenge:

A common challenge for women after childbirth is weight gain through the middle, waist, tummy, and hips. Thighs can also be a problem. For these reasons, you detest shopping. With patience, however, there are solutions.

The Solution:

In selecting tops, this petite model should go for a blouse that's cut with bigger upper-arm sleeves and wider side seams to hide the bumps and bulges. When she shops, she'll be looking for pants that fall straight off the lower part of her hips. A fuller-cut leg is what she wants.

Before

After

This blouse doubles as a jacket and covers the largest part of our model's hip. The yellow polo under it is loose-fitting and drops comfortably over the bust, sides, middle, and tummy.

It helps to buy pants that are forgiving to the hip and thigh area, cut with more room so the eye doesn't go right to the hip and thigh.

The argyle sweater—like magic—camouflages the bustline and drops straight down over the tummy. The model wears her sleeves pulled up to show more skin. You'd think she was 5'5" but she's 5'1½"! Also notice how the argyle pattern disguises the bust area.

Figure Challenges

The Challenge:

When you're short, extra weight will show in the arms, bust, middle, tummy, hips, and legs—everywhere. The model is 5'2½".

The Solution:

Petite Pluses—Be ready to look smashing in color and style! When you compare your body shape to the model here, you may notice that you have less or more weight in some areas. Still, your figure challenges are essentially the same—and the clothing styles shown here will transform you dramatically.

Clothing for Petite Plus women are out there in many choices of style and color.

Before

After

TIP:

Go to the Plus-size department and try on drapey skirts with an elastic waist.

A matching blouse like the one shown here can double as a jacket. Notice that the jacket hem ends just below the fullest part of the hip. The finished look? Absolutely lovely. These items are all Misses Plus sizes. We shortened the jacket sleeves—that's all!

The model stretched her wardrobe with a basic black knit top and a bright-colored jacket. Imagine how you can wear the same jacket and top with a well-fitting pair of black slacks or skirt.

Figure Challenges

The Challenge:

A 5' 2" lady isn't very tall, and the challenges most likely will be at every curve. My job is to re-proportion her body so clothing will have a nice flow to it.

The Solution:

First have someone take your measurements so you'll know your size. Then try on clothes in that size. You may find that you're a different size on the top than on the bottom. Dresses and skirts should be in soft, drapey fabrics that flow rather than cling to the body.

TIP:

Don't try to hide in black, black, black. Lots of colorful clothes are out there just waiting for you. Try them. Buy them.

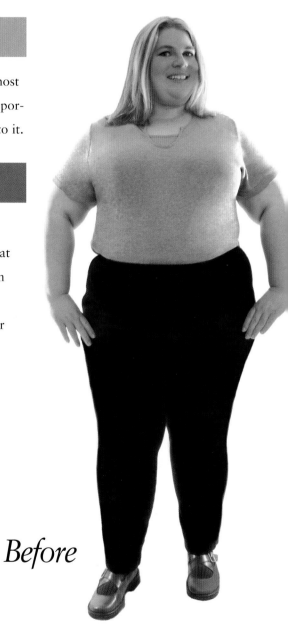

Before

After

TIP:

Some of the skirts you like won't be in Petite Plus sizes, so try on Misses sizes. They may look and fit perfectly.

The three-row block of argyle diamonds lifts our pretty blond model upward and has a slimming effect. Pushing up the sleeves a bit shows some skin and makes her look taller and more open. And don't the Petite Plus pants fit well!

She can wear a 1"-2" heel with the outfit.

Our model couldn't look any better in this colorful pink floral knit top. The side seams are cut straight so the top hides her upper body weight. The skirt has an elastic waist and drapes lightly over her hips and thighs. The hem detail in a sheer fabric complements the skirt.

Figure Challenges

The Challenge:

This petite lady will never be taller than 5', so her concerns about what looks best on her will remain the same. Our model has a larger bust than you would expect on her very small frame. You'll see how the clothing styles I chose for her minimized the bust.

The Solution:

She's barely 5 feet tall, and oh-so-tiny. When you're this small, you're thinking size "0" or size "2". The clothing style and cut of the "after" views were selected to enhance her height and show off her good figure.

Before

For the "before" shot, I asked this petite lady to wear clothing that outlined her body. You can see the knit top curve in at the sides to reveal her small torso.

After

For the Seattle bank where she works, she's wearing black pants from a brand that is cut to fit her legs, hips, and short crotch. The top, in white knit, is trimmed in black with a detachable flower. Notice that the V-neck opens up her neck and face and grows her taller.

Add to the same black pants a vertical floral print jacket that comes to life with a fuchsia top. The white knit top (left) will look great under this jacket, too. Her shoes have 2" heels.

After

TIP:

Wearing gently edgy clothes keeps you looking young, yet professional.

The fuchsia cardigan with black trim brings out the fuchsia and black print in the top underneath. She's wearing the same black pants and 2" heels.

The matching knit top with its gently curved neckline gives her a pulled-together look with the cardigan. The effect is commonly called "business casual attire." Never is her bust accentuated by what she's wearing.

After

Without a jacket, most of the model's arms show. The V-neck opens up her face. The pants are a good fit and in a fabric appropriate for the workplace—a two-way stretch that gives all-day comfort.

When her job requires a dressier professional look, she can wear this two-piece dress in navy, white, and fuchsia. Think navy jacket, navy cardigan, or off-white jacket.

The Challenge:

This model grew up with the same challenges she continues to face today. She's short in the legs, heavy in the hips, and carries extra weight in the thighs. This body is not a great candidate for short skirts, and flattering pants are hard to find.

The Solution:

I'll aim to re-proportion the model's figure with clothes that won't allow you to see her hips and thighs. Tight clothing is not the answer here! I always carry a tape measure to run across the upper pant leg, and I keep an eye out for tops that drift down over the bust, giving the illusion that everything underneath is fine!

Before

In her next life, the model wants to have longer legs and be 5 inches taller. That won't happen, so let's look at her "after" shots.

After

TIP:

Silk jackets are soft and rarely have a structured look. I like silk because the fabric drapes so well.

Here's a solution in the form of a turquoise and-black print top that fits loosely over her bust and tummy, and the black pants actually fit! A pair of strappy sandals completes her new look.

With olive skin, this model can wear a vivid shade of orange. The medium-weight, 100% silk jacket with side slits looks terrific with a brown silk T-shirt under it. The sheer lining under the skirt ends 4" above the hem to show off the lovely print.

Figure Challenges

The Challenge:

This model's primary challenge is to camouflage her hips, thighs, and upper arms. The goal will be to find clothing that covers these areas with ease.

The Solution:

Jackets should drape about 1"-2" below the fullest part of her hip. The sleeves should be cut with a larger armhole so the upper arms don't show. Pants with ample hip and thigh room will allow the pants to hang off the hip and drape over her leg.

TIP:

A petite woman shouldn't wear a shoe with a strap that wraps around the ankle. It cuts her height even more.

Before

This perky petite is only 5'1". You can see her predicament in the extra weight she carries in the hips and thighs. The upper arms become a challenge, too.

After

What fun I had getting this lady attired in an outfit to wear to an afternoon wedding! This ensemble will be just right for many evening occasions, too. Look at the colors in the jacket—there's your answer to what to wear under the jacket.

By dropping the jacket length to just above the knee, your eye misses the entire issue of hips and thighs. The jacket arms are cut with ample room so the world won't see her upper arms. P.S. Don't you just love the shoes?!

A cascade of ruffles can disguise a large bust—and ruffles are so feminine, too.

When your challenges are extra weight, stay out of Junior departments. The clothes are cute and trendy, but you'll never find a fit!

After

Here comes feminine sensuality in the form of a ruffled blouse, cascading over the bustline. The bell-shaped cuff on the sleeve adds softness, too. The black slacks with roomy legs cover the thigh area and allow our model to move with style and grace.

After

TIP:

When the pants hang straight off the hip, you can achieve a look that hides everything you don't want people to see.

She makes an effortless transition into weekend wear in an unstructured cotton jacket and pants to match. She's wearing a blue and yellow print top underneath.

Isn't this much better than sweatpants and a sweatshirt? And you can throw all three of these pieces into the washer and dryer. Notice the shoes—comfy and fashionable, too. The outfit is super for a weekend getaway. For a change, try a camisole under the jacket.

Figure Challenges

The Challenge:

At 5'4" tall, this model plays soccer and is solid muscle! The hips and thighs can move a soccer ball downfield with great agility, and her upper body is well-toned. But the athletic side of her makes it tough to find clothes for the office that are appealing on her body shape.

The Solution:

For this model, we will look for jackets that hang just below the hip, and blouses big enough to button comfortably or—better yet—knit tops. Pants should drape over the hip and tummy.

Before

The model's body shape makes me lean more toward skirts and jackets for her because that seems to be the best way to achieve an appropriate look for her muscular body.

After

TIP:

Don't give up on shopping for garments to fit your figure challenges. Retail has clothes for everyone. Every manufacturer cuts clothing differently, so ask a salesperson what brands will best fit your figure.

We found a jacket with a deeper armhole cut so her upper arms can move comfortably. The jacket length glides over her hip area, as does the fuller cut of the skirt.

Notice the skirt length—it ends at the most flattering part of the lower leg. The scarf is a nice addition, tying the skirt and jacket together. The shoes are open, which helps show more skin.

Figure Challenges

The Challenge:

The challenge of dressing this model is to play down her ample bust, hip, and tummy. We're looking for pants that are forgiving to the thighs and are roomy in the leg.

The Solution:

With a tape measure hanging around my neck, I set out to find clothes to showcase her beauty and personality. No one would ever guess the challenges we faced in finding garments to make her look slimmer and not play up the areas we're trying to play down. For one thing, the jeans don't work.

TIP: *When you're trying to downplay parts of your body, look for clothing that hangs, not clings.*

Before

After

TIP:

When you stand in front of the mirror and look at yourself from the side and front, you'll be able to make better decisions on the cut and style of clothes you purchase.

These slacks fit beautifully—dropping off the hip and giving her a smooth line up and down. The sweater jacket allows plenty of room through the bust area. The 3/4-length sleeves are flattering to her short arms, and by pushing up the sleeve even more, she will show some skin and appear taller.

Figure Challenges

The Challenge:

As a result of my cancer treatment, I lost 30 pounds. Obviously, I detest these photos, but they're staying to show how to dress to make you look heavier.

The Solution:

"Beefing up" the underweight mature lady requires layering and using bulkier fabrics. As I gain weight and fill out, I will be more pleased with my appearance.

This two-piece brown stretch knit is a life-saver for the thin petite lady. The fuller cut and drape of the skirt add bulk to your lower half. The jacket allows you to wear many different-colored knit tops underneath. Have fun with necklaces and scarves, too.

Until I re-gain my former weight, I dress to "bulk up" and make my frame look larger. The slightly wider cut in the pants and a double-breasted suede leather coat help a lot.

A flare cut on the pants gives the appearance of more weight to my legs. A heavier cardigan sweater and blouse offer a layered look that enhances my appearance.

The Challenge:

So you think this 5', 105-pound model is easy to fit? Not so fast. True, she looks trim, with firm arms and a flat tummy, but she does have a tiny bust, very narrow shoulders, a bit too much in the hip, and short legs. All her length is in her upper body.

The Solution:

Re-proportion her body. How? The jackets I chose make her torso look wider and hide her low waistline. Full-length pants with 2" or 2½" heels compensate for her short legs.

Before

After

Displaying a look of confidence, this plucky stockbroker is well turned-out in a black, double-breasted suit. The jacket ends where her hip isn't pronounced and her torso appears shorter. The gentle drape of the pants lengthens her legs.

For a look worthy of success, she's wearing a pinstripe suit. The vertical stripes add height. The pink blouse matches the stripe in the suit and frames her delicate face. Again, the jacket bypasses her waist to make her legs look longer.

Figure Challenges

Different looks for weekend wear allow you to use color and a variety of styles.

Have you ever dreamed of some of the styles and colors you can wear if you just try them out?

After

This cropped pant with an easy-to-wear elastic waist comes in washable cotton. The striped camisole shows some skin—diverting attention from her long torso. Notice that she's not wearing shoes with a strap around the ankle, as that would shorten her leg even more.

After

She's wearing the blouse collar out and turning the cuffs out over the jacket sleeves. It's a smart look for the short, petite woman with her body challenges. She's succeeded in disguising her short legs and long torso.

The black-and-white gingham-check blouse is refreshing under the white denim jacket. Together with the black capri pants, this is a casual look for the weekend as a break from her high-intensity workplace.

Figure Challenges

After

Our model is meeting her friends after work to catch up on their busy lives. How about the eye-catching sherbet-colored top, with the color repeated in the shoes! Yes, she's a Spring.

Here's a pair of basic black slacks—easy to pair with tops in a variety of colors, sleeve lengths, and necklines. Notice where this cardigan ends, giving the model the appearance of longer legs.

After

TIP:

Get creative with jewelry and shoes. Sweep your hair up and adorn it with a comb or barrette.

A strapless dress with white horizontal and vertical piping is a fetching choice for a concert or out on a summer evening. Add a black cardigan or a black or white shawl and you're all set.

Now the model is wearing a long, full skirt, topped by a wool vest with faux fur collar and black cashmere sweater. What makes her *new look* possible are the 2½" boot heels, plus the added little touch of pushing up her sleeves. If you're carrying 20 extra pounds, you'd better not try this look.

Accessories

Accessories

Accessories consist of the shoes and boots, jewelry, scarves, belts, hats, and flowers you add to clothing. Accessories are the essential touch to show off your personality. Careful accessorizing allows you to develop a style that you want to project to others.

You've seen someone coming down the street who nearly takes your breath away. Everything looks "put together!" And it is, although it does require some patience and practice.

- Leave accessorizing until you've finished your shopping.

- Take clothing pieces with you, and ask a salesperson for help.

- Many brooches, necklaces, and earrings that you've had for a long time will continue to work well for you, giving you distinction and setting you apart from everyone else.

- If you're starting to rebuild your wardrobe with new clothes, styles, and colors, you are open and ready to purchase accessories that will tastefully round out your outfits. Accessories will complete your look and give you a style all your own.

- Buy accessories that *complement* the outfit, not attention-getters in themselves.

- You don't want your accessorizing to take over the clothes you're wearing. Pins, scarves, and jewelry shouldn't be gaudy, but just the right touch to complete your "look."

Notice how you can tie the same color together in a belt and gloves to match the leather trim on the hat. Now add a black leather jacket and black boots. You're ready to take on the town!

Accessories

Accessories are actually the most important part of dressing because they show off your personality.

Shoes

After helping a client choose her clothes, I start accessorizing with shoes. When shoe shopping, carry a few garments with you to get the right look and color.

- Find shoe styles that show off your clothing to best advantage. Where do you intend to wear them? If you are on your feet a lot, comfort is a prime consideration. A wide heel that's 1" – 2" high will be comfortable all day long. Shoes with a narrow 2" – 3" heel will be killing you within hours. Manufacturers are trying hard to put out a good-looking dress shoe that is comfortable. The larger the shoe department, the better the results.

- Closed toes are best for a business look, and heels of 1", 2", or 2½" are appropriate for most workplaces that project a professional attitude. These shoes can work with pants, suits, and skirts. Rely on the salesperson for guidance.

- You may wear black shoes with black and navy clothes. Often, navy shoes are difficult to find. When I spot a pair I like, I buy them. If I wait three weeks, my size may be gone.

- When you're looking for brown shoes, you will find an assortment of shoes in various shades. Brown comes in a dark brown, a natural leather color (camel), and often a crocodile texture combined with smooth leather or a layered wooden heel.

- There are shoes to fall in love with and buy, and shoes to fall in love with and leave at the store! I have several pairs I thought I couldn't live without. Do I ever wear them? No. Sometimes my shoe addiction gets in the way of good judgment!

A 2½" heel seems high, but this is actually one of the most comfortable pairs of shoes in my closet. I can wear this shoe to shop for clients or stand and present an all-day workshop.

This is a favorite shoe of mine. It has a 3½" heel and sits in my closet, where I admire it. I've never worn this pair.

Here's a take-off on the spectator pump in navy and white. It doesn't offer much support, so wear this style when you aren't planning to do much walking.

My feet slide out of mules. Can you wear them? They go with slacks and skirts but aren't suggested with a business suit because the back is open. Consult your company's dress code for guidance.

You saw this darling shoe earlier on one of the models. It matched her outfit perfectly. When buying a new pair of shoes, you'll be surprised and overjoyed to find at times that they go with clothes you already have.

Accessories

- White shoes and spectator shoes are reserved for the summer months—the end of May through Labor Day in the United States. You may wear an off-white shoe into the winter months if the style isn't open or strappy. You'll see women wearing out-of-season shoes and clothes. Don't let that happen to you.

- Look at the photos of casual business shoes and casual shoes here. Nothing changes faster than shoe styles, so please have a shoe salesperson assist you. Be sure to ask those who have been working in women's shoe departments for at least 3 – 4 years. They really know their merchandise and which colors and styles are appropriate for the occasion.

- If you have wide feet, ask the shoe salesperson to show you shoes from manufacturers that make a wide shoe. Many designers don't cater to those needing a shoe beyond a "C" width. It's good to know which brands are going to best fit your feet. The selection and styles are better than ever now, and I hope they keep improving! There's a big market for women with wide feet.

- The woman who has a narrow foot, too, can use guidance from an experienced salesperson. The selection is often not as good as it could be, but these days there are shoes for everyone with every foot size and width. If your heel is narrow, have the salesperson insert a pad to aid the fit.

- When I see a professional woman wearing a snazzy suit, my eye travels naturally to her feet. If she's wearing a shoe that I'd wear only at home, my first impression quickly evaporates!

An off-white heel with a closed toe and back immediately tells you it's for the office—or it's just a great off-white heel!

How many times have you looked for a stylish brown heel to wear with brown slacks or a suit? Here it is with a buckle detail on the front of the shoe.

If you own blouses, tops, or skirts that have at least a touch of orange in the print, this color of shoe is hard to resist. It will spice up your outfit.

A take-off on the classic Mary Jane will perk up a dress, suit, or skirt and cardigan set.

Shop for shoes when you're not tired, and give yourself plenty of time to pick good-looking shoes that fit.

- For a dressy look, you'll find a wide array of fancy shoes with varying heel heights, from strappy to slingbacks, in different fabrics and colors.

- With casual shoes, too, the variety seems endless. Casual business footwear is a bit more dressy than a casual loafer. The dress code at your workplace will be a guide in your shoe selection here.

- Walk around the shoe department and pull five or six shoes you really like. As you do this:

  - Keep in mind what you're buying each pair of shoes for. Ask yourself: Will I be wearing the shoes for work, play, dressy occasions?

  - Know how high a heel you want to wear—and *can* wear.

- Most important, when you walk around wearing each pair, how do they feel? You need not suffer in poorly fitting shoes, ladies. Take time with your shoe buying.

- Don't try on shoes when you've been on your feet for a long time and you're tired. Your feet may be swollen.

- When the salesperson tries a super shoe on one of my clients, she says, "Now, this is happy." Then I know she's found shoes that she can walk a fair distance in any day for the life she has created for herself.

- The older I get, the more I'm willing to pay for comfort. If I'm going to spend four hours in the city shopping for a client, I know what I've got to wear that will take my feet "happily" through the day.

TIP:

Don't buy shoes just because you like them. Buy them for a purpose—work, weekends, dressy? And make sure they are comfortable.

You can wear this little cream-colored flat with a skirt and top, capris, or khakis.

You say these were on sale and you couldn't pass them up? I wouldn't either. You'll have fun wearing these shoes with animal-print clothes or as a playful accessory.

A red flat with toe decoration will be at home with jeans or capris. And even better with a red beret!

Mocha brown shoes like these will spice up your brown slacks on Casual Friday or running errands on the weekend.

You need not suffer from poorly fitting shoes. Take time with your shoe buying.

Accessories

Boots

Boots are a popular addition to footwear. Boots come in ankle, mid-calf, to the knee, and over the knee. A long skirt is "hot" with knee-high boots. Knee-length skirts, straight or flared, can be accessorized with knee-high boots. Wear opaque hose and see how you like the look.

- You may want a 1"– 2" heel. If you can handle a higher heel, they're available. A shorter boot with pants and jeans is sassy, too. It makes you want to buy a leather jacket and be the coolest lady in your neighborhood! Your shoe salesperson knows how to guide you in your final purchase. Don't forget personal comfort!

- As I browse through fashion magazines, I pay attention to models' and actresses' feet. What shoes are they wearing? Do I like the look? Many celebrities featured in credible magazines commit *faux pas*. You needn't join them. As my eye catches people in stores and on the street, this "fashion policewoman" sees what many people don't take the time and energy to do: Put the final touch on their dressing by wearing shoes appropriate to the clothes and the occasion.

- When is the last time you polished or waterproofed your shoes and boots? Do they need repairs to straps, soles, heels? Like your car, they can last many years with good maintenance.

This boot height is good with a short, flippy skirt in black. Or try a plaid skirt in red, white, and black. Wear opaque hose, a showy sweater, and turn a few heads! Do you want a higher heel? Go for it!

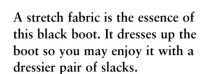

A stretch fabric is the essence of this black boot. It dresses up the boot so you may enjoy it with a dressier pair of slacks.

Accessories

Boots

The totally modern sole and heel shape make this a welcome addition to your boot collection. You can wear short and long skirts with this style. They're a natural with cords, too.

Oh, you stylish lady in this brown boot with a black swirl scattered through the leather. This one has more point to the toe and a comfortable heel.

A wider heel gives you real comfort. You're able to put a lot of walking miles on this black boot.

Can you believe an embroidered boot with the very latest in sole and heel? With fur peeking through the seams, you know you'll be warm when you wear them.

It's hard to pass up a classic Western boot, especially if you own a suede leather skirt. Another idea: Tuck your jeans into the boots and put on your black leather jacket. You'll be a hit at your country dance class!

Boots for all occasions—it's difficult to choose.

Accessories

Scarves, ponchos and shawls

Let's start with scarves. They come in an array of colors, patterns, and fabrics. There are small and large squares, and oblong short and long, wide and narrow. When shopping for scarves, take some of your tops or dresses with you to make sure the colors and fabrics complement each other. Stay away from large square, rectangular, and long oblong scarves. They can instantly dwarf you, overtaking your whole appearance. If you're short and heavyset, be careful about wearing scarves, as they add bulk to your body and make your neck appear short.

- Many women don't wear scarves because they've never learned to tie them! The salesperson can be a valuable asset in helping with your purchases and should be able to show you different ways to wear and tie them. Many accessory departments have booklets illustrating various ways to tie scarves. This will help you learn to better accessorize and use them.

- You'll need to practice tying these "little devils" because it can be highly frustrating. I can tie a square knot in a scarf without a mirror! (But I've done it 8 million times!)

A jean jacket is a common item in coat closets. Often, you'll toss it on without thinking of accessorizing. The off-white shell underneath is boring, but a small, square scarf gives it flair.

Accessory departments many times have booklets that show different ways to tie scarves.

• If you already have a drawer full of scarves, go through it and donate the ones that don't look good anymore, or the fabric is too heavy to tie gracefully, or they are "dated." Fabrics have improved so much in the last few years that you may find yourself eliminating much of your collection. The best fabrics and weights nowadays will be silk, rayon, wool challis, and better polyester. Scarves are next to your face, so if the colors are not from your color palette, give them away. Closet inventory revisited!

• Scarves often become out-of-date simply because of the fabric. Old polyester scarves tend to be too heavy and have yellowed with age. I'm inclined to get those items out of my scarf drawer and toss them. Some of the new, improved polyester scarves can be mistaken for silk. Besides, polyester is less expensive, looks good, and ties with ease.

• Shawls and ponchos are other options to complete your ensemble. As you might expect, they come in a variety of shapes, sizes, colors, and fabric variations. Peruse some fashion magazines to get ideas on different ways to wear them. I've enjoyed my shawls for evening— for warmth on my shoulders and as an elegant addition to dresses, long or short.

• Purchasing accessories is comparable to purchasing clothing: A lot depends on your budget. You can buy a small, square scarf for $18—or a designer scarf for $48 to $90. It's up to you.

This little cutie is 100% polyester. Its texture enables you to tie it as shown, and the fabric holds this look for hours. This scarf is great for a Summer lady.

Fold this lovely scarf diagonally and tie a square knot as shown. If you're a Spring, the color will be luscious next to your face.

As you invent your new personal style, you will take risks and discover how much you love the new you!

Accessories

Ponchos

Cut on the bias, this poncho has a unique feature—a hood and a zippered front so you won't mess up your hair when you put it on. And aren't the colors in the plaid super!

When I pulled ponchos for the photo shoot, this pretty one didn't go back to the store! I own it and wear it a lot with charcoal gray pants and skirts. A poncho will accessorize a lot of clothes.

TIP: *Don't buy a poncho or a shawl that has too much—or too heavy—fabric. It will overwhelm you.*

When you wear this crocheted capelet, it will warm your shoulders—and make a tasteful fashion statement besides! You may wear it just about anywhere you want.

A semi-cowl neckline and open crocheted pattern add to the richness of this poncho. The cut is asymmetrical, so I pinned up one side to reduce the fullness. You can do the same with a brooch or a decorative pin.

Try on ponchos and shawls before buying, because the length, width, and shape vary a lot.

Accessories

Shawls

Beautiful shawls add style to the garment you're wearing. Drape simply, or toss one side over your shoulder as shown at left. Often you can pin a brooch to the shawl to hold it in place.

Shawls are a must! They add a touch of elegance to your dressing. Ooh-la-la!

Fur pieces as accessories:

Wrapping a long, narrow fur piece under the collar adds a nice touch to a winter coat.

This rabbit muff has holes to slide the other side through. For $40, you'll soon get your money's worth.

Accessories

Jewelry

Jewelry is a welcome accessory—as long as it doesn't overpower and take over the clothing—and you. In general, too big, too ornate is not good for the petite lady. Avoid "busy" jewelry. It often is less expensive—and looks that way. The jewelry discussed here includes pins and brooches, necklaces, beaded jewelry, earrings, and bracelets.

Pins and brooches

- Among my most cherished possessions is a priceless collection of pins and brooches. Each has a story and a special memory behind it. You will find many of these pieces in boutiques, in antique shops, and at estate and garage sales.

- Pins and brooches can be worn on coats, jackets, and suit jackets. Often, they are too heavy for blouses and dresses. Check the weight of the fabric before pinning one on. A delicate silk will show the pinholes on your garment.

- Brooches and pins are worn on the left side of a garment. If it's a jacket or coat, pin it on the lapel—not too high and not too low.

- If you purchase or own pins with diamonds or silver, take them to a jeweler periodically for cleaning, and have the jeweler check the stones to make sure none are loose.

Each pin and brooch has a story and special memory...

This exquisite antique brooch was given to me in trade for several dresses when I had my design business. The clothes, I'm sure, are long gone, but I continue to wear the brooch.

This rich emerald green brooch is a knock-out on a black wool dress, an off-white jacket, or the lapel of a suit. Try earrings to match!

The sparkle of a semi-precious stone at the center of a brooch allows you to wear it with a simple, understated brown or black dress. My biggest challenge was finding earrings to go with it.

Glitter and pearls on pewtered gold dictate what garment will display this brooch to best advantage.

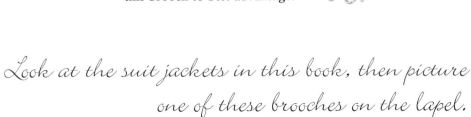

Look at the suit jackets in this book, then picture one of these brooches on the lapel.

Necklaces

The necklace is another accessory that may be lying dormant in your jewelry box. Weed out old, inexpensive pieces that no longer fit your lifestyle or the image you want to convey.

- If you have necklaces that are too long for your height but you like them, go to a jeweler who will shorten them. This is a small price to pay for a piece you'd like to continue wearing.

- Put on each of your necklaces to see if the shape, size, and length are flattering on you. Here's where an honest friend will come in handy!

- Colors in the stones, beads, and other ornaments may not look good on you now that you've determined your color palette. Perhaps your discards will go to a consignment store, or you might want to include them in your next garage sale, or maybe a friend will welcome your give-aways.

- When purchasing a new necklace, the many counters of jewelry can be overwhelming. Again, that's what the salesperson is there for. Show her the garment the jewelry will go with and tell her your price range. Explain what type of jewelry you're looking for and ask her for suggestions.

- A short, small woman needs pieces that complement her body shape. If your bust is large, don't wear a necklace with a bauble ending in the cleavage. You will find people staring at your chest. Try a little lower or higher.

This pink freshwater
pearl necklace with a blister pearl
pendant is a real eye-catcher.
Wear it with a blouse or sweater,
or with a classic evening dress.
The 23½" length is just right
for the petite woman.
This one is a
Margot Kim
design.

This 32" necklace combining gold
coins and pearls makes a nice addition
to dresses, sweaters, and blouses.

The elegant 16½" clear quartz crystal piece
with a blue lace agate pendant can
be worn with blouses, sweaters, and
dresses. It's another Margot Kim design.

*If you have necklaces that are too long for your height,
have a jeweler shorten them. It's a small price to pay.*

Beaded necklaces

For the past several years, beaded jewelry has been very popular. It comes in many bead shapes, colors, and lengths and can consist of single strands, or doubles, or triples. Get a piece that looks right on you and isn't gaudy. I've found my best pieces of jewelry at antique stores and estate sales. If you're willing to take the time and poke around, you can find priceless treasures.

- Often you can combine beaded jewelry with shiny gold or silver. Try layering a few pieces to see how you like the look. The effect can be dramatic and stylish.

- On one occasion, I wore a three-strand turquoise necklace, then layered a single-strand turquoise on top. Wow!

These are the kinds of necklaces I'm often looking for when I shop for a client. They represent an alternative to the pearl necklace and, as you can see, they can be different but, oh, so tasteful. They can be worn with many necklines, too.

TIP:

Be sure the length of the necklace is right for you. Sometimes I've taken a necklace to a jewelry store to have it shortened or lengthened so it suits me better.

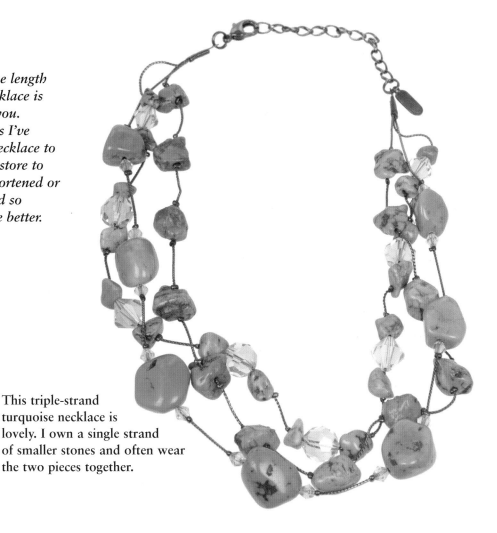

This triple-strand turquoise necklace is lovely. I own a single strand of smaller stones and often wear the two pieces together.

Try layering a few pieces to see how you like the effect. It can be dramatic and stylish.

Accessories

Earrings

Earrings are often just the right touch for an outfit, and you'll need no other jewelry. The selection in stores is immense. Ask the salesperson to help you narrow your search until you've found the right pair.

- If your ears are pierced, you have more choices than with clip earrings. If you have multiple piercings and work in a conservative environment, refrain from wearing an earring in every pierced hole!

- Reserve long dangles and ornate earrings for evening, and wear more conservative earrings to the office or on sales calls.

- Sometimes, carefully chosen earrings and a striking necklace are all you'll need to set the right tone for a dress or beautiful blouse. Wearing a ring that is a good match for the earrings is another option.

These earring sets can be worn to work.

These earring sets can be worn for evening.

Choose earrings that highlight your good taste and style.

Accessories

Bracelets

You may have fewer bracelets than other kinds of jewelry. If I'm wearing my watch, I don't wear a bracelet.

- If you wear a watch on your left wrist, wear bracelets on your right arm. Tennis bracelets are nifty, and they can be worn above or below the watch or on the other wrist. Bracelets with beads and other stones are nice, too. Price-wise, they run the gamut from low-end to high-end. Choose colors in the beads and stones that complement your clothing and color palette.

- Bracelets often come in matching sets with necklaces and earrings, but don't overload your body with all three at the same time. You can easily overdo it with too many baubles and bangles.

- Quality gold bracelets with engraving, diamonds, or other precious gems are fine accessories. You may find these locally or when you travel to another country. Hammered and pewtered silver with set-in stones of turquoise make a beautiful fashion statement. Often, these pieces are inherited, and you will leave them to someone special when you pass on. They are timeless. Enjoy!

TIP:

When you consider wearing more than one bracelet, put on one to four bracelets at a time and jiggle your arm. If the bracelets make a lot of noise and you don't want to call attention to yourself, cut back to only one of your favorites. Are you going to an interview, the movies, the opera, the symphony? Say a definite NO to extra clutter and noise! If you're out for the evening, layer your wrist ware.

A hand-engraved silver bracelet might be years old, as shown here, or you may purchase something like this, new.

Gold bracelets in different widths and textures are classy. I often wear three of these at the same time. They're all old and were gifts from special people.

Bracelets often come in matching sets with necklaces and earrings, but don't overload your body with all three at the same time.

Accessories

Hats

Hats—Can you wear them? Do you wear them? If so, what do you wear them for and to? Personally, I adore hats, and I own a variety of them. They're a snappy "add" to my personality. Besides, they cover up a "bad hair day."

- Winter hats, summer hats, baseball hats, beautiful hats for suits, dresses, weddings, funerals. Hats for fun. It's your choice, but you'll need to spend some time in front of the mirror to see what looks good with the shape of your face and hairline.

- When you select a hat, keep your color palette in mind, along with what you plan to wear with the hat.

TIP:

Try on several hats to find the best shape for your face.

A pink fedora—why not?! Cock it to the side a bit, turn down the brim on the left side, and wear with jeans or a pant suit to look chic. This hat is well-suited for winter because it's made of felt.

Here's a pretty, wide-brimmed straw hat for summertime. The brim is a bit wide, so make sure you don't get buried under it. If you're 5'3" to 5'4", you can pull it off.

This jaunty little suede-leather cap can be worn with jeans or cords and a jean jacket or a leather coat.

Isn't the color of this hat positively yummy? And the high crown, offset by the narrow brim, will make you look taller. This may turn out to be a terrific look for you.

Winter hats, summer hats, baseball hats, beautiful hats for suits, dresses, weddings, funerals. Hats for fun.

Handbags

Most women carry a handbag. When I think of all the things I must have with me when I meet with a client, I know exactly what kind of space and partitions I want when shopping for a new bag. Handbags are highly personal. They must fit your criteria. As you look at the handbags pictured here, you'll notice that none is gargantuan. A petite woman doesn't want to tote around a suitcase-size bag. Just as in big, baggy clothes, you can get consumed by the size.

How about a colorful handbag to spark up a navy or black ensemble? This leather bag doesn't allow room for a lot of extra stuff. Be honest: How much do you really need to carry?

When you consider buying a bag with two-toned detail, be sure it works with enough clothes to make it worth your purchase. This one zips totally shut to keep your possessions safe. That I like.

- When picking out a new handbag, first ask yourself how much you are willing to pay. Good-quality handbags run the gamut from $50 up to hundreds of dollars A really nice leather bag is typically $150—$250. If you're not willing to part with that kind of money, other bags cost less, and often you can find your "perfect bag" on sale.

TIP:

Before shopping for handbags, ask yourself: Do I want a hand-carry bag or do I want a shoulder strap?

Grommets are prominent now, and they announce that you're smart and sophisticated. The inside of this leather bag has several zippered compartments— designed for safekeeping. This is great for travel, too.

Here's a basic black leather handbag for daytime wear. This one will work equally well with business or casual attire, and you'll be able to carry it with lots of different clothes.

Accessories

Evening bags

When you purchase an evening bag, you normally have in mind an outfit to wear it with. You're headed to a party or an event when evening purses are appropriate. You'll want to keep them for many years, simply because you don't use them nearly as much as day bags. And, oh! the memories and secrets these little creatures carry with them!

- Most often I'm not going to carry that much inside an evening purse—a credit card, some cash, tissues or hanky, lipstick, a small mirror, and a comb.

- The color in evening purses can bring out a sparkle in your dress or complement a necklace and earrings. Different shapes and sizes are bountiful.

- If you're looking for a gift for a friend, first get a peek at her wardrobe of evening wear, then check out the variety of silver and gold clutches, as well as other colors and finishes. Sparkly handles or a beaded design might attract your eye.

Oh, my! For evening, here's a gorgeous gold satin bag in an attractive shape. The tassel is a sweet touch. You can use the shoulder strap or tuck it inside.

I fell in love with both of these bags, so we photographed them together. Now you can decide which size and shape you like best—a clutch to hold with your hand or the handled one that gets carried along. You won't go wrong with either of these!

Black satin is so stylish, especially with a satin bow and large, sparkly decoration. A shoulder strap is tucked discreetly inside if you want to use it.

This charming pink satin bag has a clasp opening and a double bow near the top. Wear it with a long, black gown—and heels the same color in satin. Nice!

Accessories

Belts

Because I suggest that the short, petite lady limit her wearing of belts, I'm not showing many of these. You may enjoy wearing a black belt with black pants or jeans or a leather-colored belt with blue jeans, and you certainly can wear a narrow belt that has no design with dress slacks.

Less and less often do you find dress slacks with belt loops. This makes a statement: No belt loops, no belt.

Here's a chain belt with a nifty fastener. It can be worn on the outside of a top—good accessorizing!

TIP:

Belts should be no wider than 3/4" to 1½" for the petite lady.

This display includes a belt with grommets and one with jewels.

Clothing for
the petite woman
under 5' tall

Clothing for the petite woman under 5' tall

Dressing the woman who is shorter than 5 feet is probably the most overlooked area in clothing. This unfortunate circumstance is driving this segment of the population into Junior departments. If you're a grown woman over 25 years old wanting to look mature and professional, you're in for some challenges! But it *is* getting better. The Gap has announced that it is adding a "professional clothing look" to its stores. By the appearance of the garments, The Gap is on target! When I visited the store, it had great slacks in Junior sizes and another rack with the same pants in shorter lengths. I'm noticing a wider selection for Petites in many stores. Hallelujah!

When you go to a store's website, you may see clothes to order online. Even though I discourage catalog buying while you're finding your way to a new style and quality, this may be a positive avenue for the under-5-foot woman.

One client is a career woman in her mid-30's who is 4'10" and weighs 95 pounds. It didn't take me long to realize her problem! She works in a well-known Seattle bank and must look professional every day including Casual Friday, when employees have the green light to dress down for Friday but still remain professional in attire. Her size in retail is a "0", or sometimes a size 2 or 3, depending on the manufacturer. I found dress pants at The Gap that are suitable for business wear. In Macy's, I found suits in the Junior department with a very professional look and great fabrics. Ann Taylor and Ann Taylor Loft have a good Petite section. So does Talbots.

If you go online before your shopping trip, you'll find many stores that offer Petite sizes. For example, Banana Republic and J. Crew are offering some good looks in jackets, pants, and suits. Most often your sleeves and pant hems will have to be shortened—that's a given at your height.

TIP:

Ask store managers when they'll be getting new shipments of the type of clothing you're looking for. The very small sizes "0" and "2" go quickly. Get on their phone, e-mail, and mailing lists. Don't miss out!

At Macy's, I went to the Petite department and pulled size "0" in blouses, pants, suits, and jackets. In some cases, blouses and knit tops were labeled "XS" (extra small), and that worked fine. Sears and Penney's have made great strides in their Petite departments. As you explore, you will gain valuable information that will turn you into a savvy shopper for your tiny frame.

When I needed more blouses for my client to try on, I went to the Misses department and pulled blouses with 3/4-length sleeves. Brilliant, I thought! This length for sleeves in blouses and jackets has been shown for a couple of years—a boon to the short, petite woman. Notice that many jackets have a slit at the bottom of the sleeve, allowing you to simply turn up a hem and avoid alteration costs—another improvement in clothing design and construction.

You still must be careful with your choices in pants, especially jeans and cords, which often have embroidery on the legs and even the seat of the pants. That will transform your look into a hip teenager when your age is well beyond that—not a professional look in the workplace. Always refer to the dress code of your company, and adhere to what your employer expects.

Don't get upset if alterations are needed to shorten jacket sleeves and pant hems. Many of you sew and can do your own alterations. If not, stores have personnel who are ready, willing, and able to do this for you. The under-5' petite lady will find helpful suggestions throughout this book for necklines (no turtlenecks, short gals!), jacket styles and lengths, and more.

Tricks of the trade

Tricks of the trade

- Inexpensive clothes *look* inexpensive. The quality of fabric and the workmanship don't look as good as finer clothing, and the garment won't hold up as well as one that costs more.

- If you've been buying less expensive clothes, bump yourself up to the next level of price and quality and see how much better the garment looks and feels. If you can't afford it now, make that a goal to work toward. I'm not pushing you into expensive, high-end clothes. Just go a level higher, even if you have to buy fewer clothes for now. Promotions happen at work when you're dressed looking like a good candidate for advancement.

- By the time they're 14 years old, many females are already looking at the body type that will be theirs for the rest of their lives—aside from weight fluctuations. Long arms will never get shorter, and vice versa. Heavy calves can be streamlined somewhat with exercise, but they still won't look slim. An oversize bust will require attention to finding a good-fitting bra and garments cut for your bust size. Flat hips or heavier, fuller hips are challenges for some women all their lives.

- Aside from cosmetic surgery, you'll be looking for ways to dress your body shape to accentuate the positive and deemphasize the negative aspects of your figure.

- You may like it. You may hate it. But it's *you* every morning when you look in the mirror! If you're small on top and large on the bottom, you'll be looking for ways to balance the proportions. The same is true if you're large on top and small on the bottom.

Tricks of the trade for the pear-shaped woman

Let's talk about the *pear-shaped woman*—small on top and large on the bottom. If you're small on top, your bust size may be only a 32 or a 34, A or B, and your shoulders will be narrow, which makes your hips and thighs look larger. Now let's re-proportion.

- Search for tops with a horizontal stripe or a pattern that makes your torso appear bigger.

- Wear sweaters and knits with a wide neck that stretches to the edge of your shoulders. This makes your shoulders appear wider.

- To add dimension to your torso, select ribbed-knit tops.

- Add 1/4" to 1/2" shoulder pads so your narrow shoulder line will appear proportional to your hipline.

- Dolman or raglan sleeves with shoulder pads disguise narrow shoulders. By contrast, set-in sleeves emphasize the narrowness of your shoulders because the shoulder line of the garment is falling off your shoulders.

- Call on your alteration professional. I've watched these wizards tweak garments and, like magic, give a whole new look to what you're wearing.

Tricks of the trade for the inverted-triangle woman

The problem of the *inverted-triangle woman* is the opposite of the pear-shaped body. Your bust is large, your shoulders are wide and square, and perhaps you're carrying extra weight on top. You'll want to minimize your torso. In blouses, look for soft, silky fabrics and knit tops that aren't fitted and therefore drop down over the bust and don't cling to your sides.

Be honest. Your undergarments make a big difference in how your clothes look. You might realize that it's time to purchase a new bra that fits you better. Try a minimizer bra. It will take inches off your bust and you'll notice the improvement right away.

On the bottom, your hips are small and you'll want to wear pants that are proportional—pants with a boot cut (bell bottom) versus a straight, slim-cut leg, which accents your upper body all the more. The flair in the pant leg helps balance your look. Also, a fuller pant leg takes the attention away from your hip area (which has mysteriously disappeared) and blends better with your topside.

Voila! You've passed Camouflage 101.

Look in the mirror to see what you've accomplished to counter the inverted triangle or pear shape. Basically, you add to one place and take away from another place on your body to give the illusion of a well-proportioned shape! Every time I look at a new client, I ask myself, "Where and how am I going to re-proportion this lady so she looks good?" You can do it yourself!

Other tricks of the trade

- Please—no deep V's or cleavage for your business clothes. Whether you have a small or a large bust, try on different necklines to see which are modest yet flattering.

- If you're close to ideal weight, try knit tops that are slightly curved or fitted at the side seams. If the fit is good and not too tight, this cut can slenderize and enhance your body shape and make you appear taller.

- Be wary of full turtlenecks. There's too much fabric around your neck, which will look bulky. They also convey negative body language that makes you appear less open, less responsive—all closed in. A mock turtleneck will work better.

- Blouses come in patterns, florals, plaids, and plain colors. They may be sleeveless, short-sleeved, or long-sleeved. Necklines range from V-shaped to rounded and square shapes. Some have a collar and lapels, and others have a mandarin collar that buttons all the way up to the neck. Again, you might be attracted to a design, but stop and consider how it looks on you. There are garments you can admire but shouldn't wear.

- Wear pointed-toed shoes versus square-toed shoes. Or a front that has a narrow-square toe or a toe that tapers.

- Be as objective and honest with yourself as you can. If you have a friend on whose judgment you can rely, invite her to give you a friendly but truthful critique.

- When trying on a garment that doesn't appeal to you, ask yourself:

    - Is it the collar?

    - Is it the cut of the sleeve?

    - Is it the color?

    - Is it the rib or finish of the fabric?

    - Is it too long?

    - Is it too short?

    - Is the print too big?

Two or three of the above should be enough for you to move on to the next piece of clothing.

These are tricks of the trade that I call upon all the time with clients. They're the nuances that make a big difference in appearance. You'll pick up on these tricks while you're trying on different clothes and styles.

Not everything I pull for a client will work. We simply keep moving along. You can do the same. If you don't like the look of a piece of clothing, move on. Don't let a salesperson talk you into it. You'll end up returning it, or the garment will hang in your closet forever—with the price tag still attached!

TIP:

A cloth tape measure will make shopping a breeze. Toss it in your purse so you'll have it when you need it. Stretch a tape measure across any body area, and that will tell you whether the garment goes to the dressing room or stays on the hanger.

If you have a friend on whose judgment you can rely, invite her to give a friendly but truthful critique.

The new you

The new you

For now, in your new venture, try on clothes and get a sense of what works for you in terms of style, color, texture, and weight of fabrics. If you're a catalog buyer, these factors are sometimes hard to determine. When you get an idea of your style, find catalogs that cater to your new look. If you've made a deal with yourself to upgrade the quality and look of your clothes, you will have to drop some catalogs and send for different ones. Hiding in oversized dresses, pants, and tops will no longer do. No matter what your size, you deserve to look great!

- When you're looking at clothes in stores, be alert to new styles and fabric combinations. You may have been in a rut for a long time. Are you beginning to look out of date? Too old? Too frumpy? Too matronly? Too young? With new information and a better selection of styles and fabrics, you will be pleasantly surprised by what retail stores have to offer. Your same old look is still out there, so ask for some help from salespeople. Tell them what you *don't* want, and ask for brands that will bring you up to date with a fresh, new appearance. A 24-year-old who wants to look professional still wants an edge to her clothes but doesn't want clothing that says she's still in junior high or high school. Whatever the age, I sneak in a bit of an edge with all my clients.

- You may choose to stay away from shopping for clothes in stores where you used to shop. If you expect to find

something new and refreshing, it probably won't be in the "old you" places. You may want to pick several new stores that cater to a look you'd like to explore. This is an adventure!

A woman 48 to 54 years old doesn't want a matronly look. By the same token, stay out of your daughter's closet.

- Getting a new hair color and cut can put you in a better mood to shop. I go with clients to the salon and sit through the new cut and color before we go clothes shopping. Your "new hair" will prepare you for new clothing and the *new you*.

TIP:

When you've finished shopping, organize your closet. Put your knit tops and blouses together. Hang your pants on good pant hangers. When you hang sweaters, too often they stretch and get out of shape—growing longer and longer. Gently fold your sweaters and put them on shelves where you can see them.

The new you

Ruts to avoid

Ruts to avoid

Women sometimes dig themselves into a rut—mainly because they haven't a clue what looks good on them. This "clothes thing" takes thought and hard work. If you detest shopping, that's understandable. There's a ton of "stuff" out there. Decisions. Decisions.

Are there ugly clothes in retail? Yes—unfortunately, plenty! There will always be clothes I wouldn't choose for anyone. Here goes with some ruts.

1. **Jumpers** – They're generally cut with a plenty of room so you can hide a multitude of sins. But you're going to look frumpy in oversized longer jumpers or dresses that tie in back. Avoid these styles at all costs, please! Oversized jumpers have no style, and there's nothing flattering about them. They have become a cop-out for a lot of women.

2. **Leggings** – They're definitely not flattering. They show every bulge and bump in your lower body. Besides, they're outdated. Are they found in retail? Yes, but it doesn't mean you're going to buy them. If you've been in that rut, don't go backward and purchase new leggings. I used leggings on the "Before" shots of some of the the models to make the figure challenges apparent.

3. **Sweats** – Retail offers some good-looking sweat styles and fabrications, but keep them for working out at the gym or running to the grocery store, not for work—and definitely not for casual business attire. A frequent topic in my workshops is "Workout Wear" and it's not in the dress code of most companies.

4. **Oversize sweatshirts** – Most of us have one or two oversize sweatshirts. Mine go to the swimming pool or the gym—that's it!

5. **Bib overalls** – Either long- or short-legged bib overalls are not a feminine look—and they're definitely a poor fashion statement.

6. **Oversized blouses** – Oversized blouses are not for petite women. The oversized shirt will dwarf you, push you down, and make you look shorter. Leave oversized blouses for the tall gals who can carry off the look with their long legs.

7. **Tight-fitting clothes** – If you're a tiny-framed, short, petite woman, avoid wearing clothes that are highly structured and fit snugly. They make you look smaller and shorter, and you're already small and short. Grow a taller look in the new clothes you choose. By the same token, tight-fitting clothes on a busty or hippy woman are not appealing.

Clothes to avoid

- In the workplace, avoid frills, laces, and flounces if you're over 30, as these make you look like you're dressing too young. If you're in your 20s, ask yourself or the salesperson if the garment would be appropriate for the workplace.

- Trendy, cutesy, and too young are not for the work environment. It's a sad commentary when a woman continues to dress like she did in high school just because her measurements are the same. This is where I've helped many a woman achieve an up-to-date look that's not matronly and still has an edge.

- Some clothes are ideal for "after five" but not work. If you're planning to go out after work, take the appropriate clothes and change after work. Don't assume that your co-workers will overlook the obvious—that you're overdressed. This mistake can even cost you a promotion or a raise.

This raincoat is much too long and heavy for the petite woman. But take a hint from the choice of color in the scarf, which complements the deep burgundy in the raincoat. A shorter version of the same style may work for you.

ELLEN YORK IMAGE INSTITUTE

With such a huge collar on this raincoat
and the voluminous amount of fabric,
it clearly would be a poor choice.

Boots worn with the raincoat should be
knee-length. The "just above the ankle"
boot cuts your height, making you look
much shorter.

A huge, bulky sweater with a big pattern is
not flattering on the petite woman. Too big
and too long is not a good look on your
short frame.

Ruts To Avoid

Helpful hints

Helpful hints

- If you're having trouble determining your best colors, find a reputable person to analyze your colors before you start shopping for clothes. The first thing I do with new clients is to color-drape them. Too many women have a closet full of black or, worse yet, every color of clothes imaginable, trying to figure out what colors look best on them. A salesperson who has been in the business of make-up application could be of help here.

- If you despise shopping, as so many women do, ask a friend to go along, or call an image consultant in your area and get some help. The investment is well worth it.

- Many times your breasts are hanging so low that nothing fits properly. Buy three good-fitting bras. This will make a tremendous difference in how your blouses, knit tops, and sweaters look on you. Ask a fitter in the lingerie department to help. Depending on the clothing you wear, you may want to buy one bra with a little padding so your nipples don't show through your garment. Often, clients' bras are in such bad shape that I steer them first to the lingerie department. A trained salesperson knows what size you should wear.

- Pick two or three basic colors for your pants and skirts. Then buy five tops for each pair of pants or skirt—and eventually two jackets for each pant and skirt.

When people are talking with you, their eyes are on your face and hair before they check out what you're wearing. So what's next?

- After color-draping my clients, the next step is to get your make-up done by a professional and learn how to apply it. You'll notice that your make-up has the same colors as your swatch card from the color analysis.

- Put your face in the hands of a make-up expert, who can enhance any face with a few good touches. Staying up-to-date on make-up and application techniques will enhance your natural beauty and improve your self-esteem.

- Practice applying your new make-up. It should take no longer than 10 minutes every morning. The proper make-up is an essential finishing touch to accentuate your assets. A natural look is what most women want these days.

- Get a spiffy new hairstyle, and perhaps some color highlights for a more youthful look. If you and your hair stylist have gotten in a rut, check out someone new. When people are talking with you, their eyes are on your face and hair. They will notice and compliment you.

TIP:

Buying new clothes is one improvement. Getting a new hairstyle and color is a must, along with new make-up.

Helpful Hints

- Mix and match. Having a lot of clothes doesn't mean you have a functional wardrobe. Mixing and matching will give you a much wider selection and you won't get bored with your clothes. When you have blouses and knit tops that can work with two or more different skirts or pants, you're on the right track. Moving jackets around between skirts and pants is a sign that you're getting the mix-and-match idea.

- If you want a turquoise blouse, buy a turquoise knit top, too. It will expand your wardrobe possibilities. Wear the blouse one week and the knit top the following week.

- Keep in mind that personal shoppers employed by a store limit their shopping to only the store where they work. An image consultant shops anywhere and everywhere, always with her clients' best interests in mind.

- If you wear glasses, buy a new, modern frame that will enhance the shape of your face. So many people buy new clothes and don't bother with new eyeglass frames. Wake up, ladies—it's time to live and make some changes!

- Slumped or narrow shoulders? Set 1/4"– 1/2" shoulder pads in your garments to elevate your shoulder line and give your shoulders some shape.

- Wear control-top pantyhose to enhance the look of your pants at the hip and tummy. If you don't like or don't wear pantyhose, department stores sell several styles of control panties that will aid the appearance of your tummy and hips.

Common-sense suggestions:

• Look at silk, rayon/polyester, linen/polyester, linen/rayon, rayon, and wool blends. If you choose 100-percent polyester fabric, you'll feel too hot or too cold because this fabric, even the new polyester, doesn't breathe. Another problem with polyester is that perspiration stains are difficult to remove and perspiration odors often won't come out even with washing or drycleaning. If you have a problem with perspiring, go to a lingerie department and ask for sweat guards. You'll save your garments in the long run.

• When you buy natural fibers such as silk, cotton, wool, and linen, you'll feel comfortable because these fibers breathe. They hold up better and require less care.

• You can hand-wash most silk garments if the quality of the fabric is good. Visit a fabric store or department store and ask for a soap that's used for hand-washing silk garments. Don't forget to read the instructions!

• If you purchase an outfit of linen in combination with another fabric, it will look better and wrinkle less. Linen/silk and linen/rayon are good combinations and will make your garment "behave" better. Linen does wrinkle, and the constant upkeep can be tiring. It doesn't travel very well either. Many of the recent knit fabrics are great because they wash and dry well, and they travel well, too.

Helpful Hints

Your wardrobe

Your wardrobe

"I have a lot of clothes and nothing to wear!" Are you in this trap? Use the key below to unlock the secret to a wardrobe that lends itself to your career and lifestyle. One list is for the career-oriented closet, and the other is suggested for the casual wardrobe. In the more casual wardrobe, please don't go over the edge to grunge and sloppy. Perhaps that's what you're moving away from.

Business Wardrobe	Casual Wardrobe
• 2 – 3 jackets	• 2 – 3 casual jackets
• 3 pairs of pants	• 3 pairs of jeans
• 6 blouses	• 1 – 2 pairs of cords
• 6 knit tops	• 1 – 2 pairs of capri pants
• 2 – 3 sweater sets	• khaki pants
• 2 tailored skirts	• T-shirts (in your best colors, long- and short-sleeve)
• 2 soft skirts	• vest
• 2 dresses	• sweaters and sweater sets
• 3 – 4 pairs of shoes	• blouses—cotton and blends (prints, stripes, plaids, and plain colors)
• appropriate jewelry	
• raincoat	
• warm coat	

After you lay out the dollars to build your basic career wardrobe, gradually add to it with new jackets, pants, and tops. Clothes on the above lists will take time and money to acquire. Be patient. Allow a few hours each time you shop. When you get tired—STOP!

A plan of attack

Each season you'll want to add pieces to your closet. Every year you'll need to get rid of clothes that are starting to look worn and you no longer wear. We all make mistakes, and I don't like to see those mistakes hanging in my closet knowing that I can't stand the style, fit, or color. When you go from your cold-climate wardrobe to the warm and hot seasons, do a quick inventory and dispose of items you no longer wish to keep. Closet inventory revisited.

For workshops, I pull 10 to 14 garments from a department store to demonstrate how few clothes are needed to build a fully functioning wardrobe. When you start your journey to looking great and purchasing new clothes, your closet will take on a new, appealing look. You'll be excited to get up and dress every day. That's what you want—nifty clothes that make dressing every day easy and fun instead of ho-hum drudgery.

Walk through stores and study mannequins dressed in clothes that appeal to you. Ask a salesperson for help in assembling several outfits that mix and match. Go to other stores to fill in the blanks so you will emerge with a different look that has style and adds dimension to who you are. Look for clothes that fit your career and lifestyle—vacations, entertainment, dinner parties, and perhaps a new social scene you're building for yourself!

When you've finished shopping, organize your closet. Put your knit tops and blouses together. Hang pants on good pant hangers, and gently fold sweaters and put them where you can see them. When you hang sweaters, they tend to stretch and get longer. You don't want that! Fold sweaters and put them on shelves in your closet.

I help arrange clients' closets so they will look forward to getting dressed and going about their day knowing they look terrific. Having dressed and outfitted many satisfied clients over the years, I predict that you will face the world with more confidence and a sense of pride in yourself after applying what you've learned from this book.

A final word: Before you rush out on a shopping spree, don't feel compelled to spend a lot of money right away. Start with a few basics, and budget for new pieces every month. Soon your wardrobe will be a pleasing sight and you'll be enjoying the fruits of your hard work and your newly acquired shopping skills.

Let the text and pictures you find in this book be a source of your success. Good luck!

—Ellen York